THE BEST OF
EAGLES
FOR GUITAR

ISBN: 978-1-5400-3017-7

HAL•LEONARD®

Visit Hal Leonard Online at
www.halleonard.com

Contact us:
Hal Leonard
7777 West Bluemound Road
Milwaukee, WI 53213
Email: info@halleonard.com

In Europe, contact:
Hal Leonard Europe Limited
42 Wigmore Street
Marylebone, London, W1U 2RN
Email: info@halleonardeurope.com

In Australia, contact:
Hal Leonard Australia Pty. Ltd.
4 Lentara Court
Cheltenham, Victoria, 3192 Australia
Email: info@halleonard.com.au

STRUM AND PICK PATTERNS

This chart contains the suggested strum and pick patterns that are referred to by number at the beginning of each song in this book. The symbols ⊓ and ∨ in the strum patterns refer to down and up strokes, respectively. The letters in the pick patterns indicate which right-hand fingers play which strings.

p = **thumb**
i = **index finger**
m = **middle finger**
a = **ring finger**

For example; Pick Pattern 2
is played: thumb - index - middle - ring

Strum Patterns

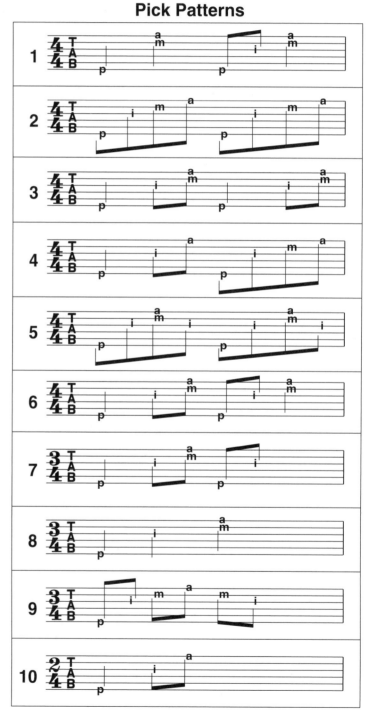

Pick Patterns

You can use the 3/4 Strum and Pick Patterns in songs written in compound meter (6/8, 9/8, 12/8, etc.).
For example, you can accompany a song in 6/8 by playing the 3/4 pattern twice in each measure.
The 4/4 Strum and Pick Patterns can be used for songs written in cut time (¢) by doubling the note time values in the patterns. Each pattern would therefore last two measures in cut time.

After the Thrill Is Gone

Words and Music by Don Henley and Glenn Frey

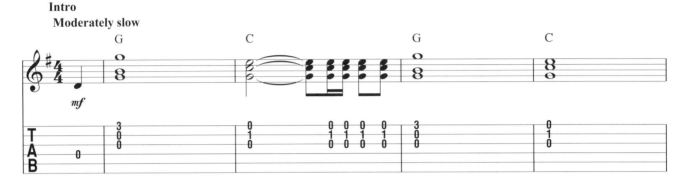

Strum Pattern: 5
Pick Pattern: 1

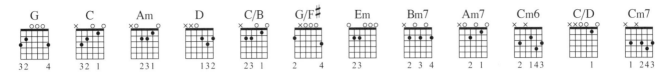

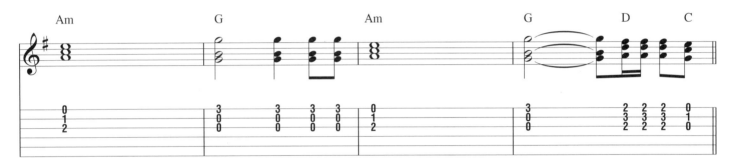

1. Same danc-es in the same old shoes. _ Some _ hab-its that you just can't lose. _
2., 3., 4. *See additional lyrics*

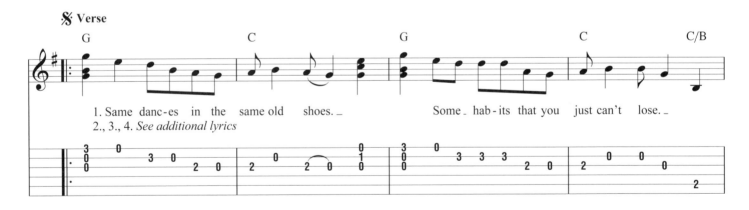

3rd time, to Coda 1
4th time, to Coda 2

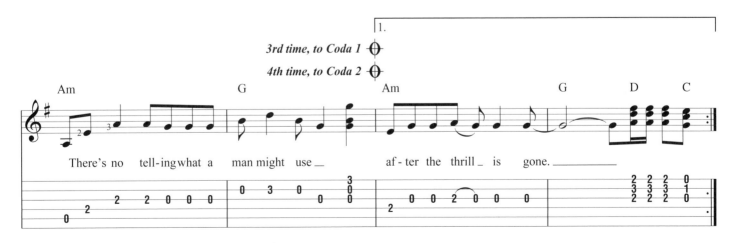

There's no tell-ing what a man might use _ af-ter the thrill _ is gone. _____

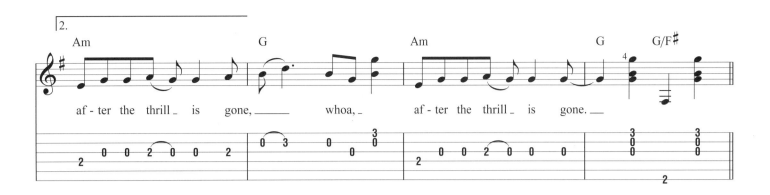

Bridge

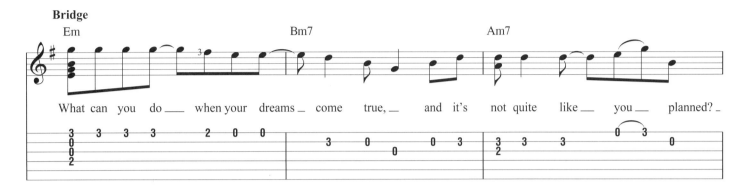

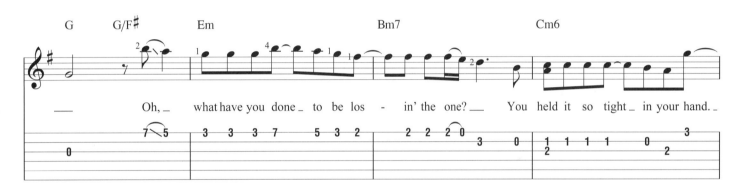

D.S. al Coda 1 $\oplus$ **Coda 1**

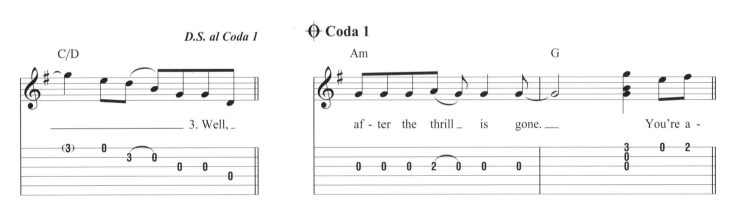

Bridge

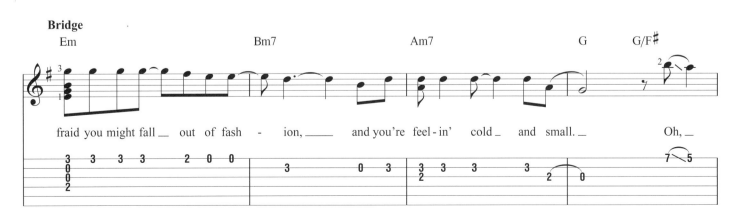

Em ... Bm7 ... Cm6

an-y kind of love _____ with-out pas - sion, _____ that ain't no kind of lov - in' at all. _____

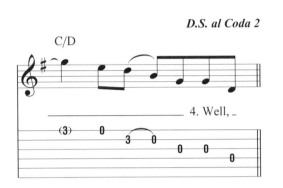

D.S. al Coda 2

C/D

_____ 4. Well, _

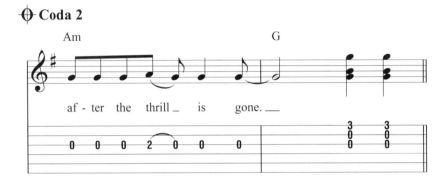

Coda 2

Am ... G

af - ter the thrill _ is gone. _

Outro

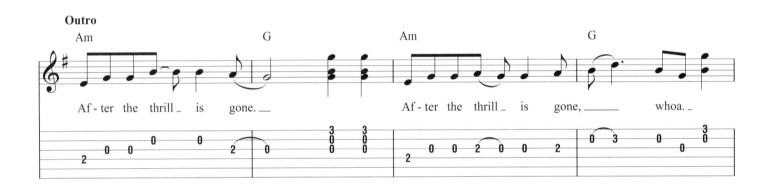

Am ... G ... Am ... G

Af - ter the thrill _ is gone. _ Af - ter the thrill _ is gone, _____ whoa. _

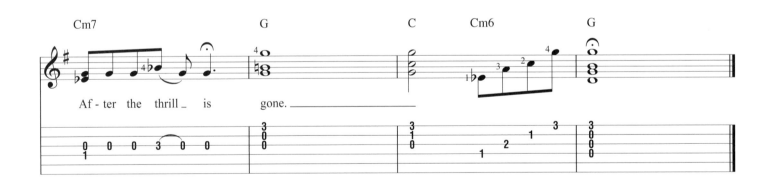

Cm7 ... G ... C ... Cm6 ... G

Af - ter the thrill _ is gone. _____

Additional Lyrics

2. The flame rises but it soon descends.
   Empty pages, and a frozen pen.
   You're not quite lovers and you're not quite friends
   After the thrill is gone, whoa, after the thrill is gone.

3. Well, time passes, and you must move on.
   Half the distance takes you twice as long.
   So you keep on singing for the sake of the song,
   After the thrill is gone.

4. Well, same dances in the same old shoes.
   Get too careful with the steps you choose.
   You don't care about winnin' but you don't wanna lose
   After the thrill is gone.

I Can't Tell You Why

Words and Music by Don Henley, Glenn Frey and Timothy B. Schmit

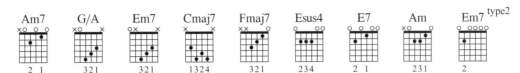

*Capo II

Strum Pattern: 1, 3
Pick Pattern: 3

Intro

Moderately slow

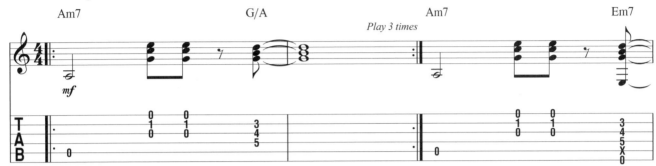

*Optional: To match recording, place capo at 2nd fret.

Verse

1. Look at us, ba - by, up all night. ___
2. *See additional lyrics*
3. *Instrumental*

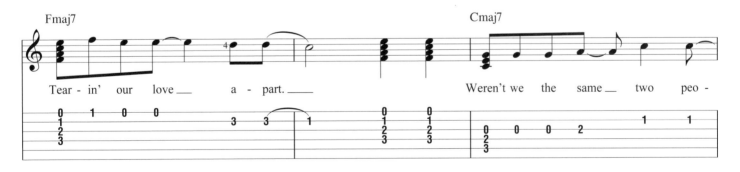

Tear - in' our love ___ a - part. ___ Weren't we the same ___ two peo -

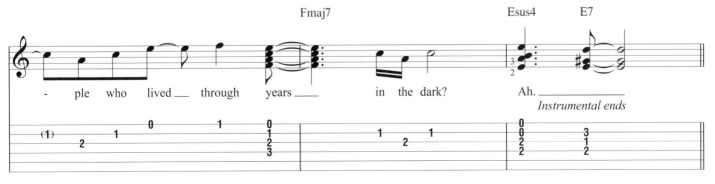

- ple who lived ___ through years ___ in the dark? Ah. _____

Instrumental ends

Chorus

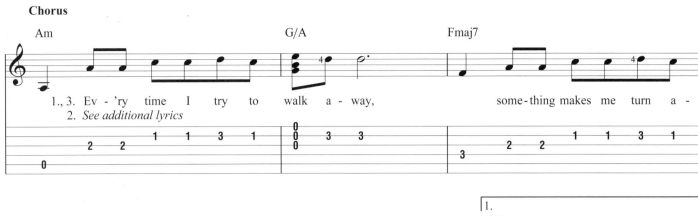

1., 3. Ev-'ry time I try to walk a-way, some-thing makes me turn a-
2. *See additional lyrics*

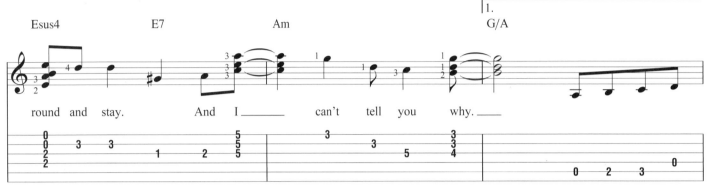

round and stay. And I _____ can't tell you why. _____

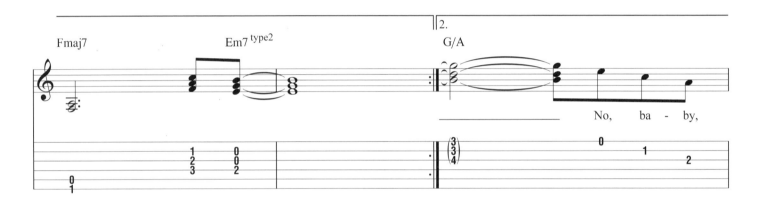

No, ba-by,

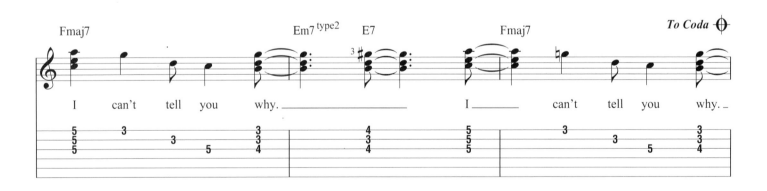

To Coda ⊕

I can't tell you why. _____ I _____ can't tell you why. _

Interlude

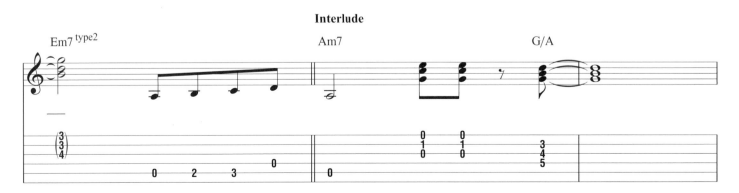

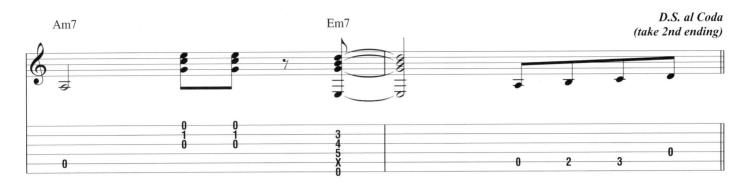

Coda

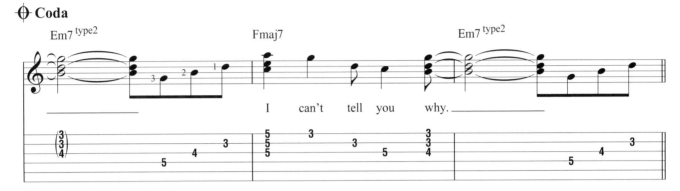

I can't tell you why. _____

Outro-Solo

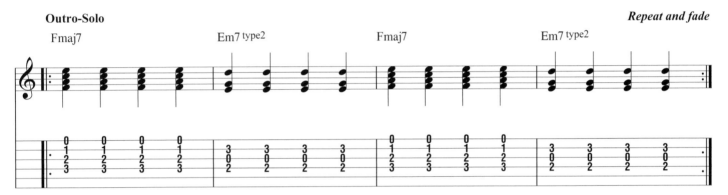

Additional Lyrics

2. When we get crazy, it just ain't right,
   Girl, I get lonely, too.
   You don't have to worry, just hold on tight
   'Cause I love you.

Chorus 2. Nothin's wrong as far as I can see.
   We make it harder than it has to be.
   And I can't tell you why.
   No, baby, I can't tell you why.
   I can't tell you why.

Already Gone

Words and Music by Jack Tempchin and Robb Strandlund

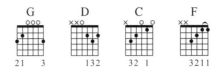

Strum Pattern: 1
Pick Pattern: 5

Intro
Moderately fast

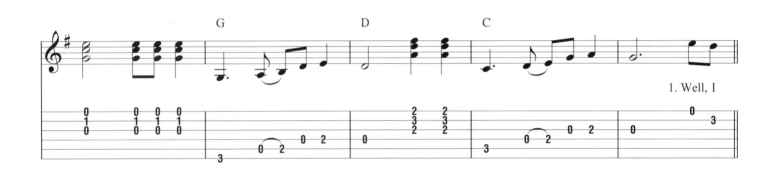

1. Well, I

%. Verse

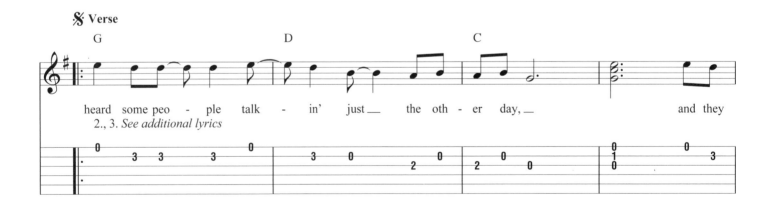

heard some peo - ple talk - in' just ___ the oth - er day, ___ and they
2., 3. *See additional lyrics*

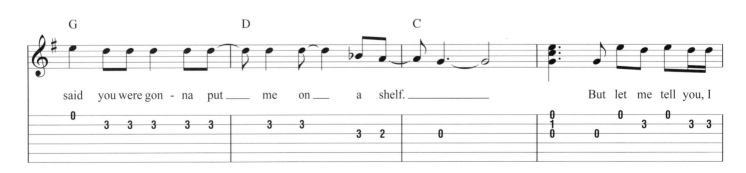

said you were gon - na put ___ me on ___ a shelf. ___ But let me tell you, I

got some news__ for you,_____ and you'll soon__ find out it's true,__ and then you'll

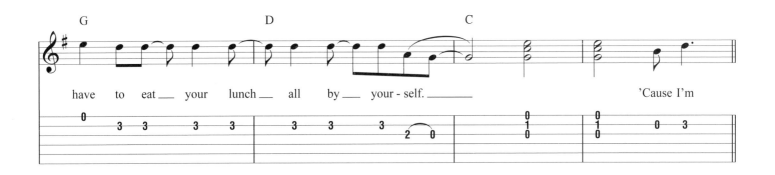

have to eat__ your lunch__ all by__ your-self._____ 'Cause I'm

Chorus

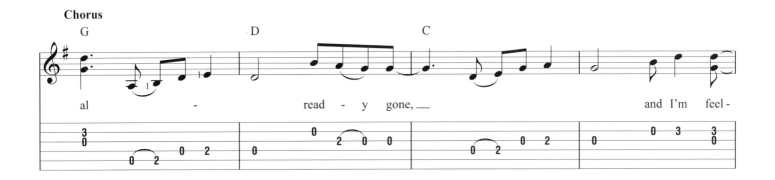

al - read - y gone,__ and I'm feel -

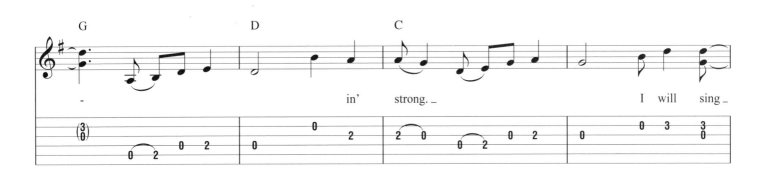

- in' strong.__ I will sing__

3rd time, to Coda ⊕

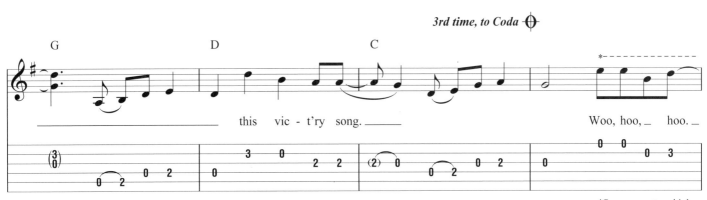

this vic - t'ry song.____ Woo, hoo,__ hoo.__

*Sung one octave higher.

D.S. al Coda

Coda

Outro-Chorus

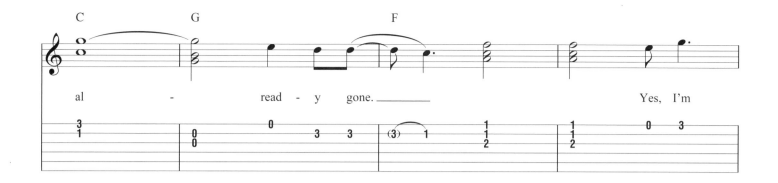

al - read - y gone. _____ Yes, I'm

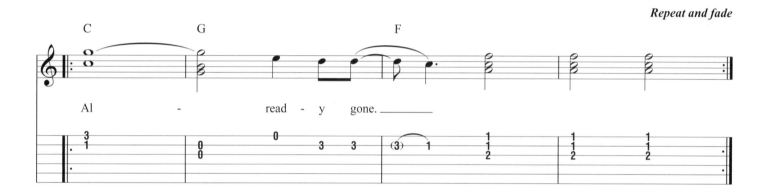

al - read - y gone. _____

Repeat and fade

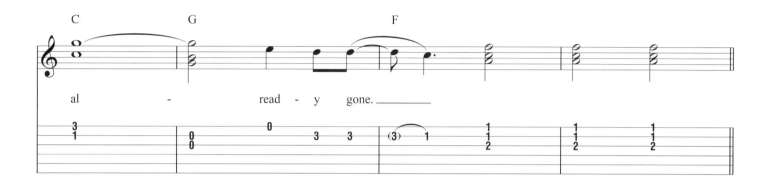

Al - read - y gone. _____

Additional Lyrics

2. The letter that you wrote me made me stop and wonder why,
   But I guess you felt like you had to set things right.
   Just remember this, my girl, when you look up in the sky:
   You could see the stars and still not see the light. *That's right.*
   And I'm...

3. Well, I know it wasn't you who held me down.
   Heaven knows it wasn't you who set me free.
   So often times it happens that we live our lives in chains,
   And we never even know we had the key.
   But me, I'm...

Best of My Love

Words and Music by Don Henley, Glenn Frey and John David Souther

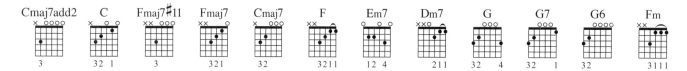

Strum Pattern: 1, 2
Pick Pattern: 2, 3

Intro
Moderately slow

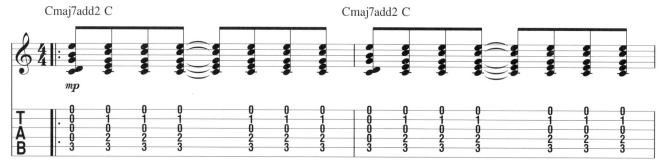

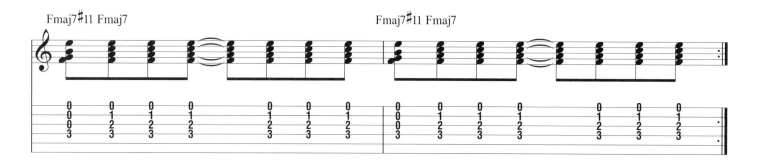

𝄋 Verse

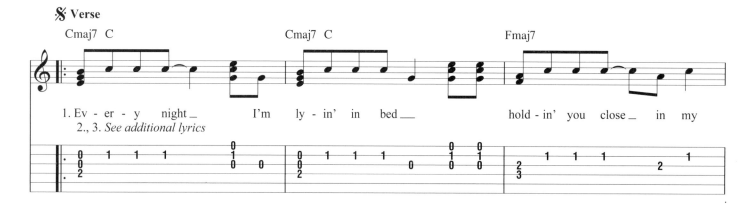

1. Ev - er - y night __ I'm ly - in' in bed __ hold - in' you close __ in my
2., 3. *See additional lyrics*

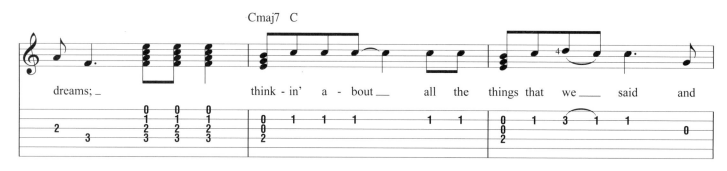

dreams; __ think - in' a - bout __ all the things that we __ said and

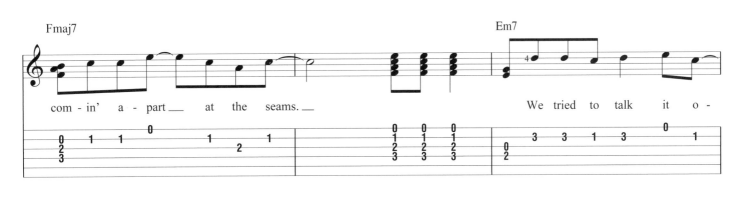

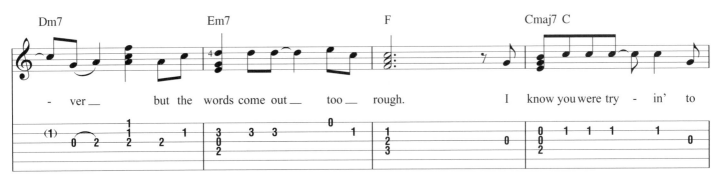

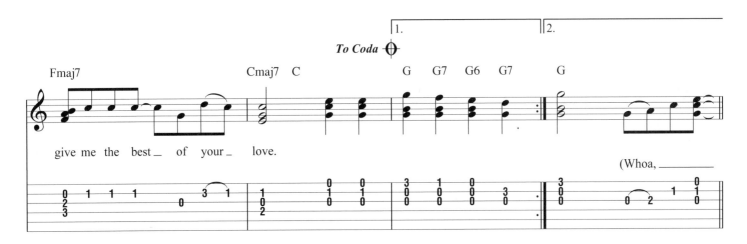

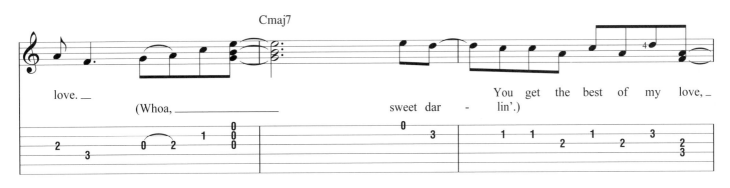

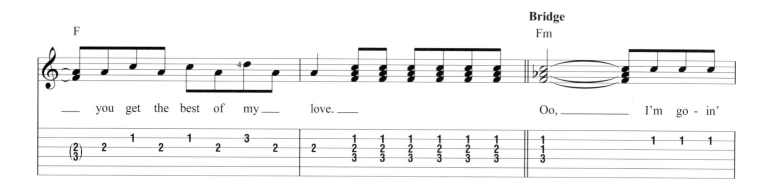

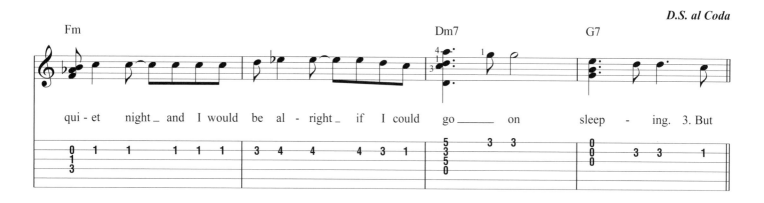

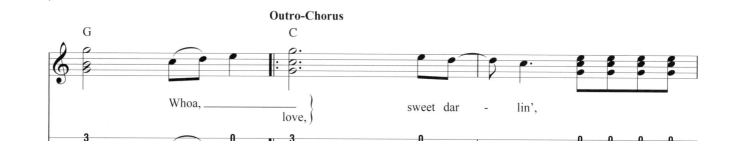

Coda

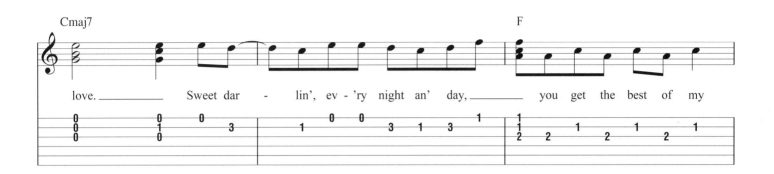

Additional Lyrics

2. Beautiful faces an' loud empty places, look at the way we live;
Wastin' our time on cheap talk and wine, left us so little to give.
That same old crowd was like a cold dark cloud that we could never rise above.
But here in my heart I give you the best of my love.

3. But ev'ry morning I wake up and worry what's gonna happen today.
You see it your way and I see it mine but we both see it slippin' away.
You know we always had each other, ababy, I guess that wasn't enough;
Oh, oh, but here in my heart I give you the best of my love.

Desperado

Words and Music by Don Henley and Glenn Frey

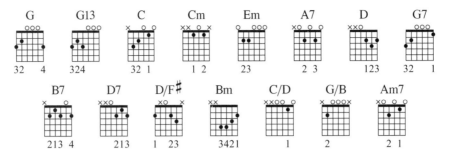

Strum Pattern: 3, 4
Pick Pattern: 4, 5

Intro
Moderately slow, in 2

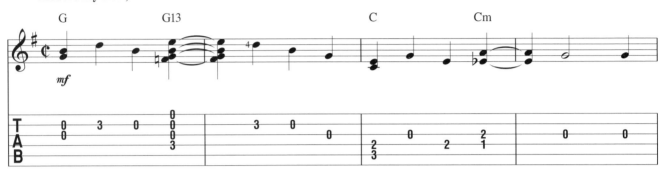

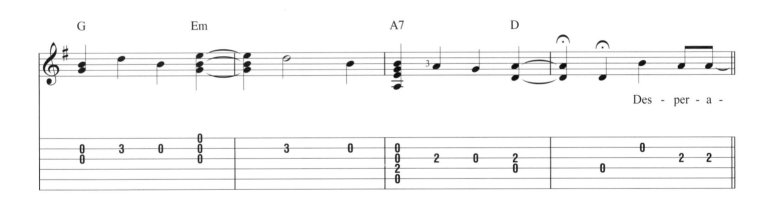

Des - per - a -

Chorus

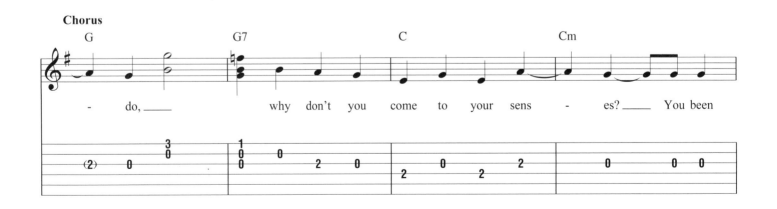

- do, _____ why don't you come to your sens - es? _____ You been

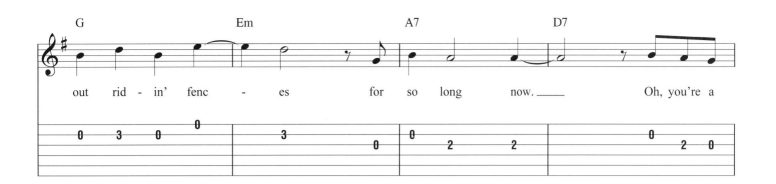

out rid - in' fenc - es for so long now. _____ Oh, you're a

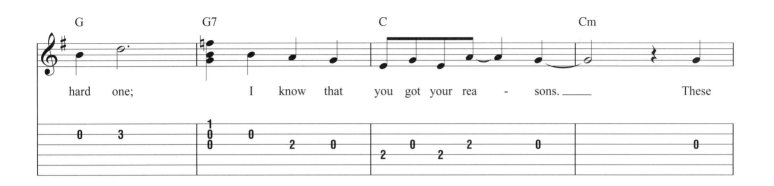

hard one; I know that you got your rea - sons. _____ These

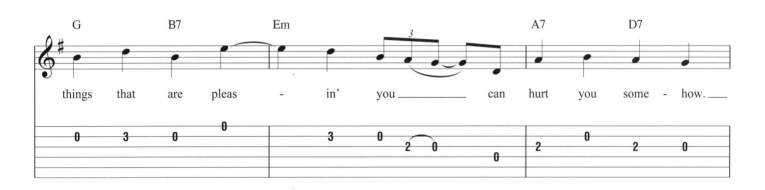

things that are pleas - in' you _____ can hurt you some - how. _____

Verse

_____ 1. Don't you draw the queen _ of dia - monds, boy, _ she'll

beat you if she's a - ble. _____ You know the queen of hearts _ is al -

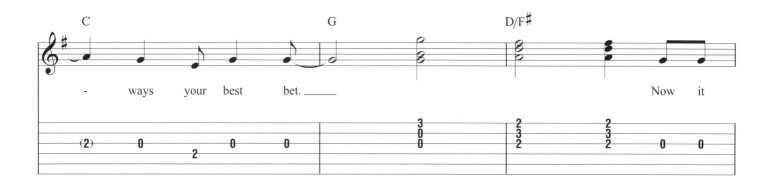

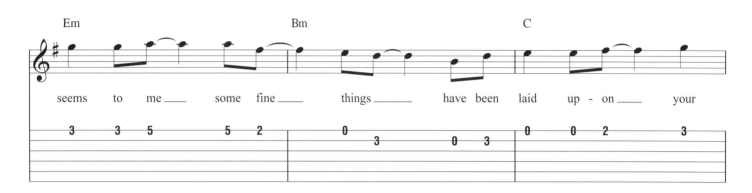

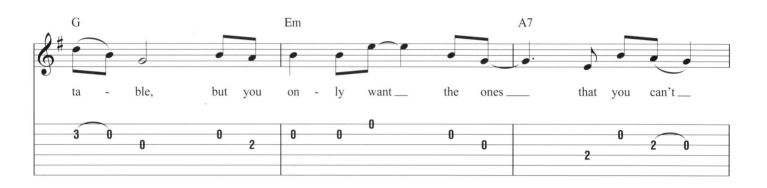

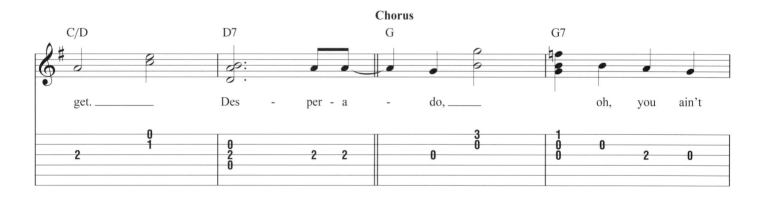

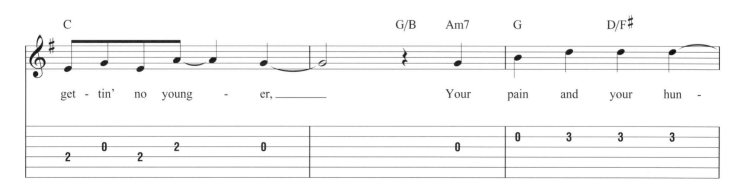

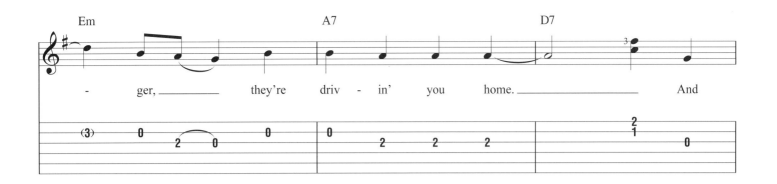

-ger, _____ they're driv - in' you home. _____ And

free - dom, _____ oh, ___ free - dom, ___ well, that's just some peo - ple talk - in'. ___

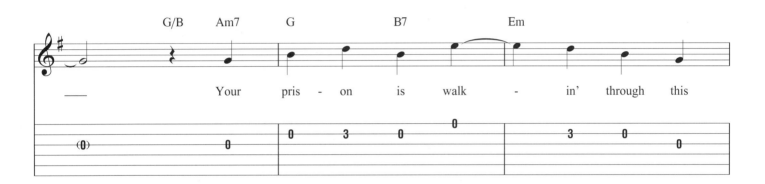

___ Your pris - on is walk - in' through this

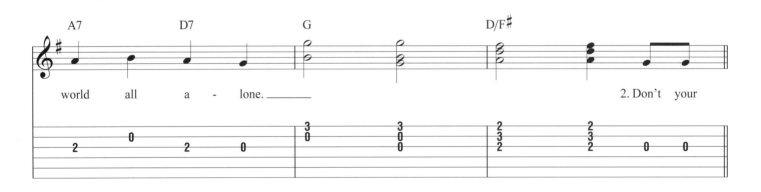

world all a - lone. _____ 2. Don't your

Verse

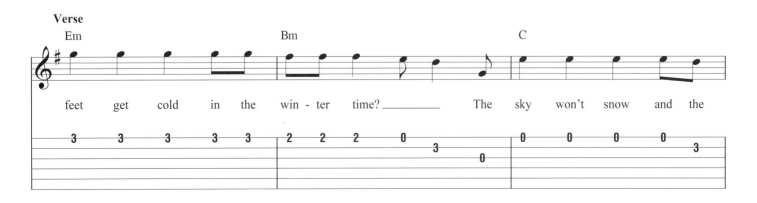

feet get cold in the win - ter time? _____ The sky won't snow and the

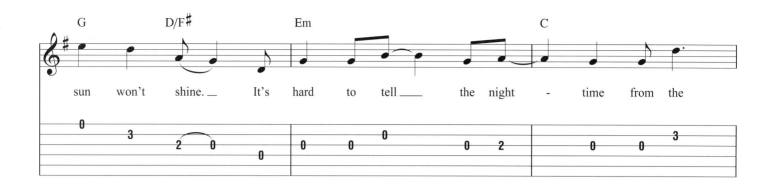

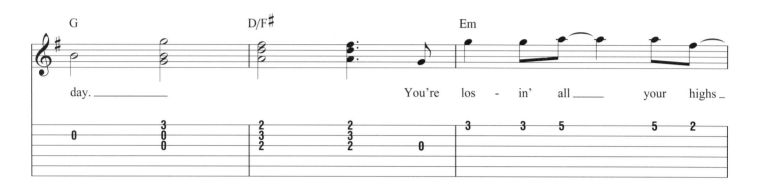

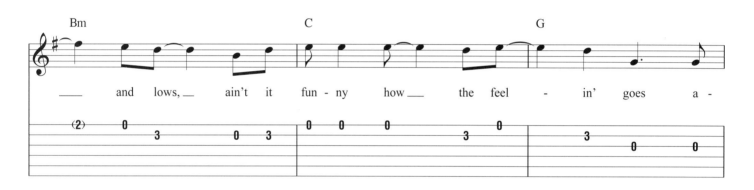

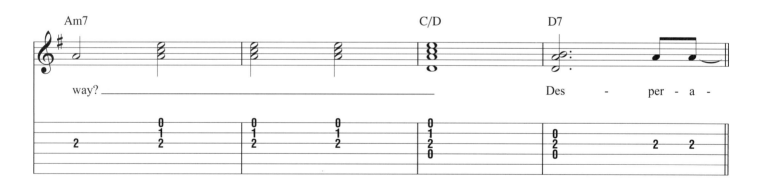

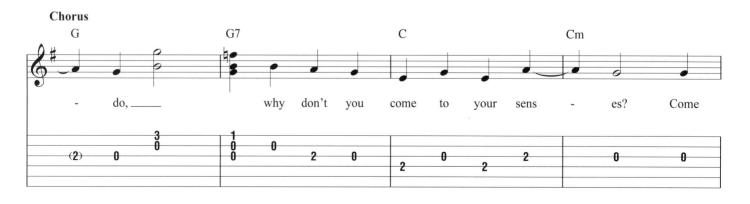

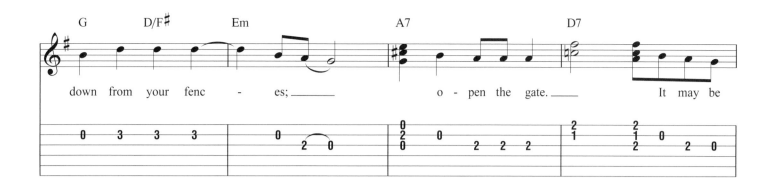

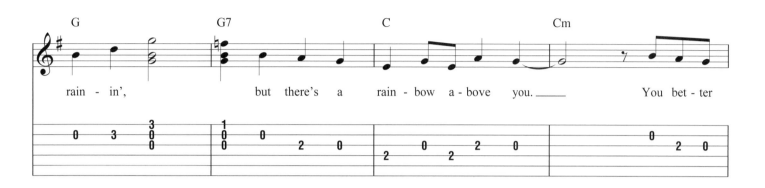

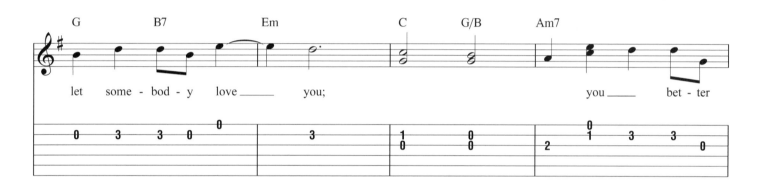

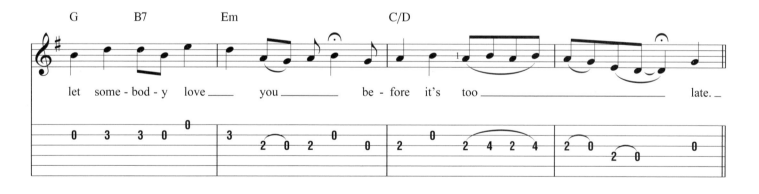

Outro

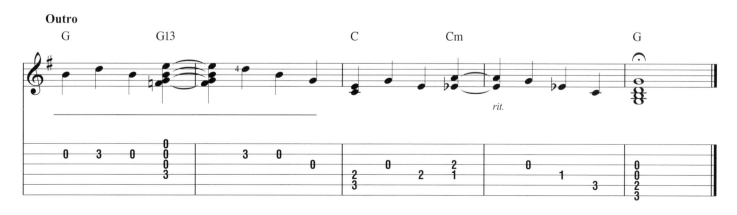

Heartache Tonight

Words and Music by Don Henley, Glenn Frey, John David Souther and Bob Seger

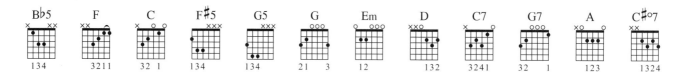

Strum Pattern: 1
Pick Pattern: 5

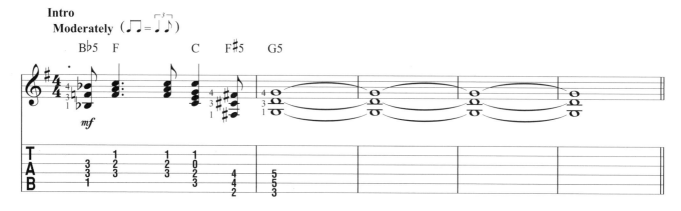

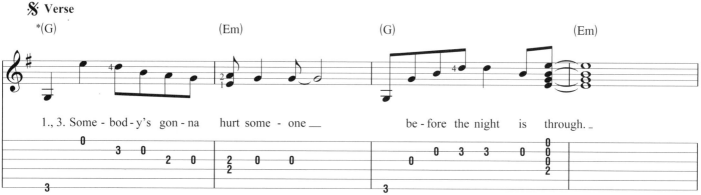

*Chord symbols in parentheses reflect implied harmony.

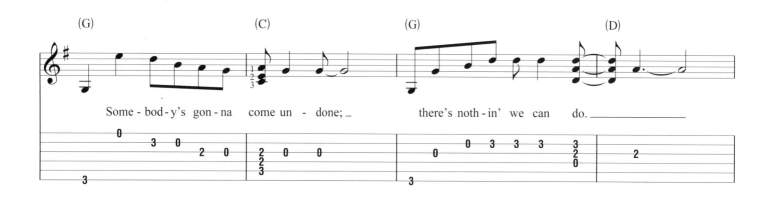

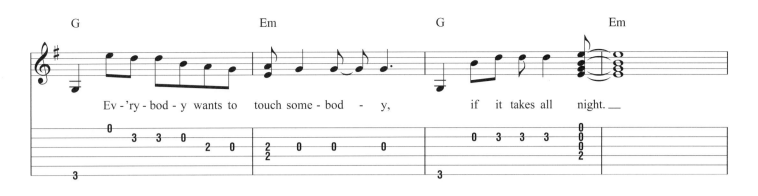

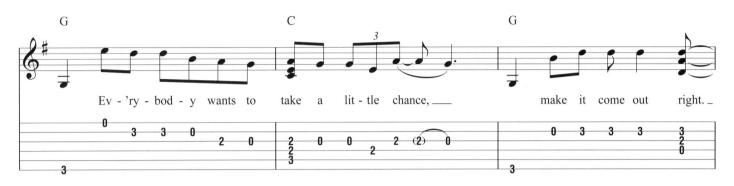

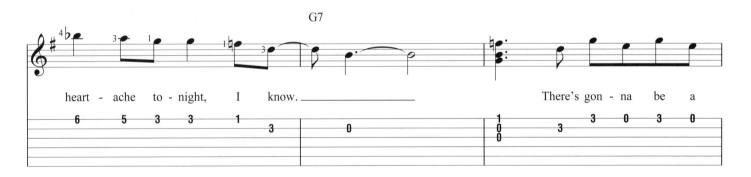

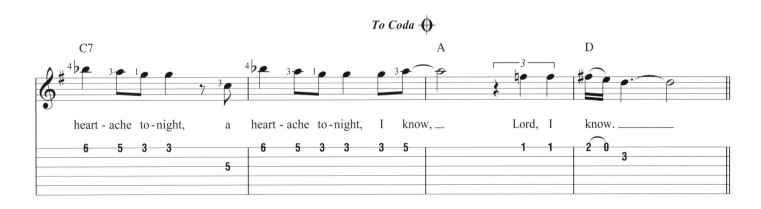

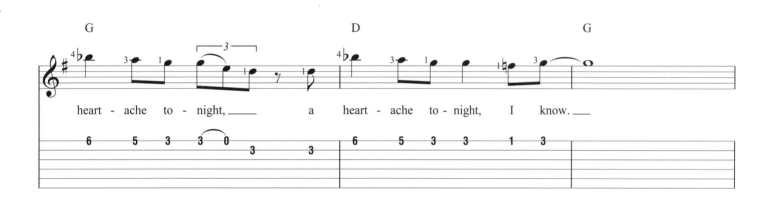

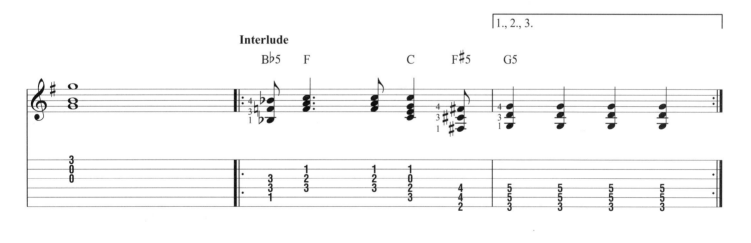

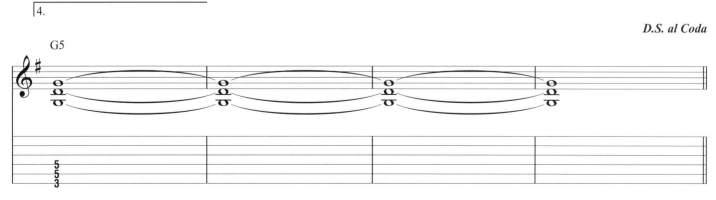

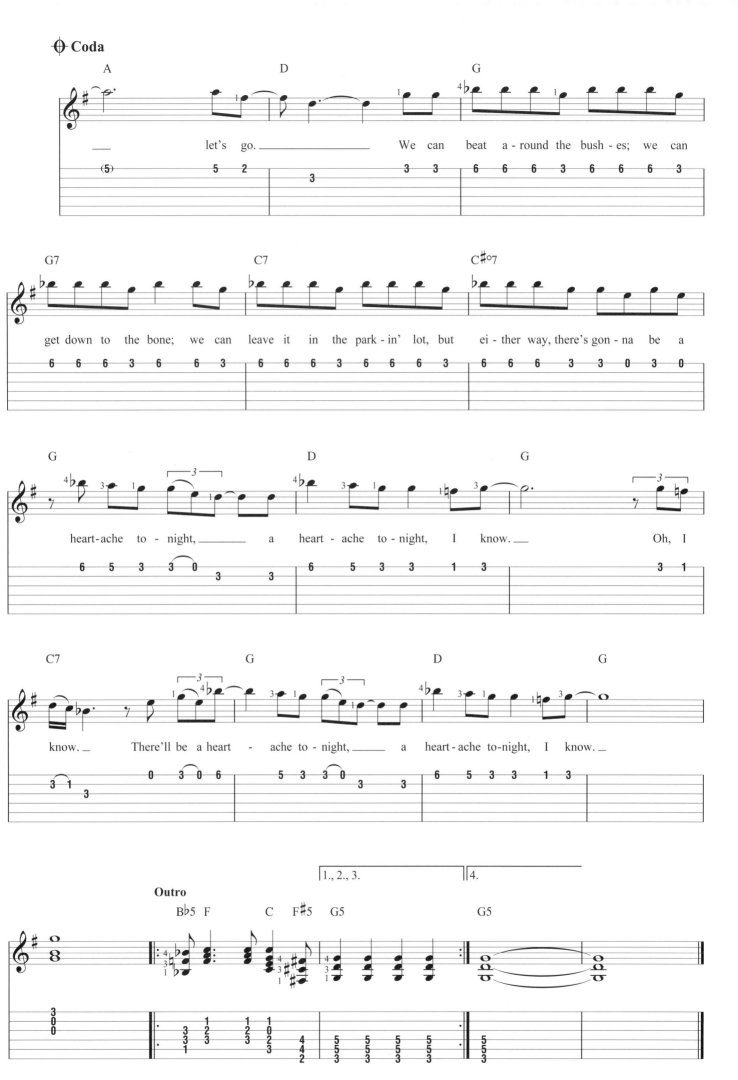

Hotel California

Words and Music by Don Henley, Glenn Frey and Don Felder

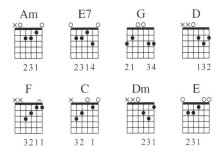

*Capo II

Strum Pattern: 3
Pick Pattern: 4

Intro
    Moderate Rock, in 2

*Optional: To match recording, place capo at 2nd fret.

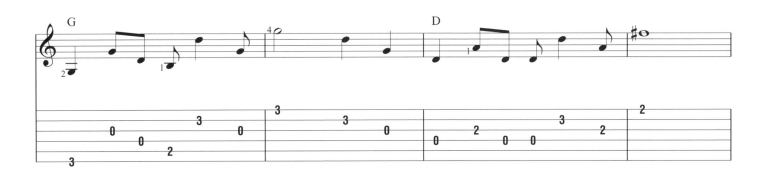

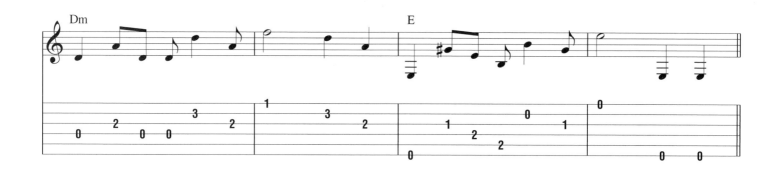

𝄋 Verse

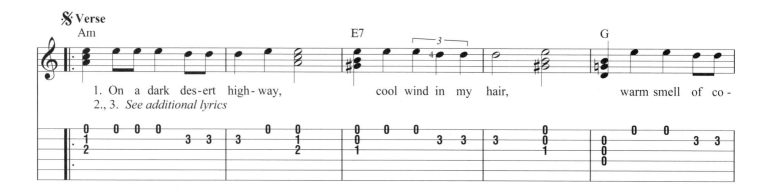

1. On a dark des-ert high-way,   cool wind in my hair,   warm smell of co-
2., 3. *See additional lyrics*

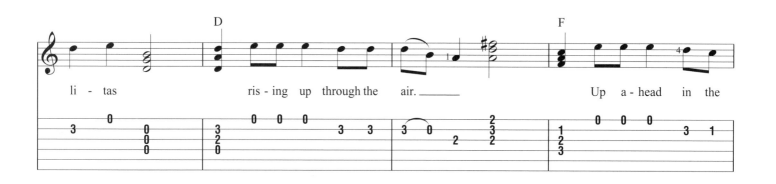

li - tas   ris - ing up through the   air. _____   Up a-head   in the

dis - tance,   I saw a shim-mer - ing   light.   My head grew heav - y   and my

sight grew dim; _   I had to stop for the   night.   There she stood   in the

door - way; I heard the mis - sion bell. ___ And I was think-ing

to my - self: ___ this could be heav - en or this could be hell. ___ Then she lit up a

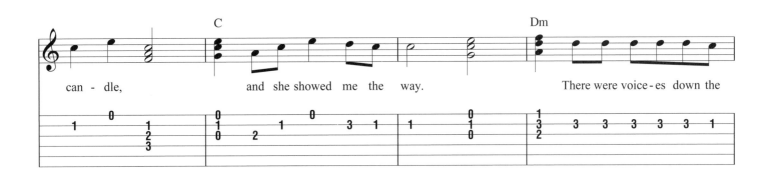

can - dle, and she showed me the way. There were voic-es down the

3rd time, to Coda 𝄌 **Chorus**

cor - ri - dor; ___ I thought I heard them say: "Wel - come ___ to the Ho-

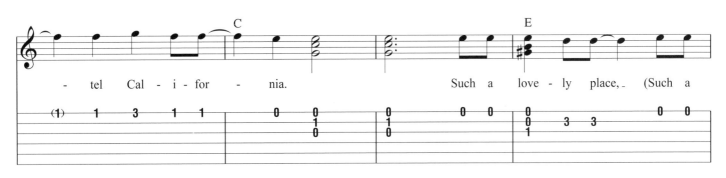

- tel Cal - i - for - nia. Such a love - ly place, (Such a

31

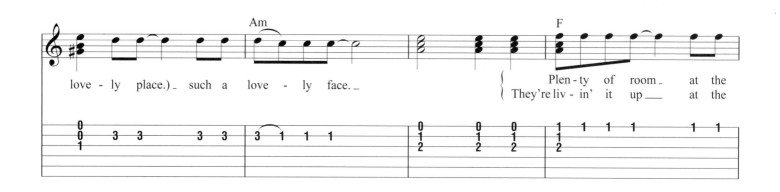

love - ly place.)_ such a love - ly face. _   Plen - ty of room_ at the
                                                     They're liv - in' it up ___ at the

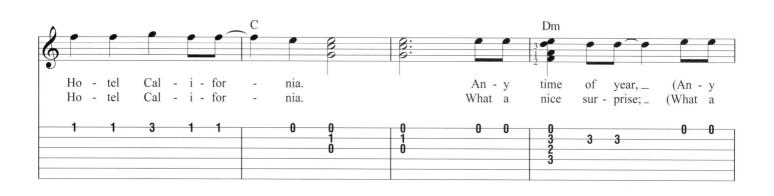

Ho - tel Cal - i - for - nia.   An - y time of year, _ (An - y
Ho - tel Cal - i - for - nia.   What a nice sur - prise; _ (What a

time of year.)_ you can find it here."   al - i - bis." _____
nice sur - prise.)_ bring your

D.S. al Coda

⊕ **Coda**
Outro

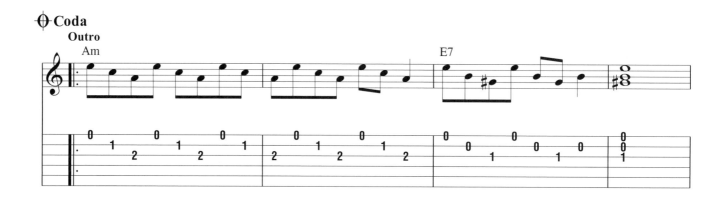

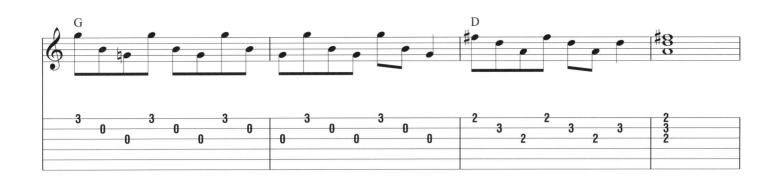

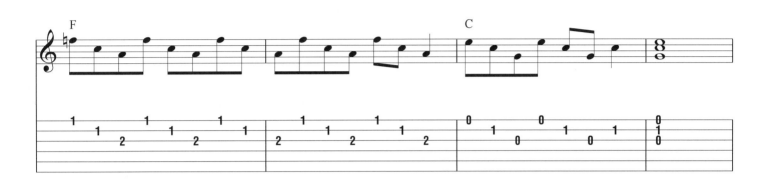

Repeat and fade

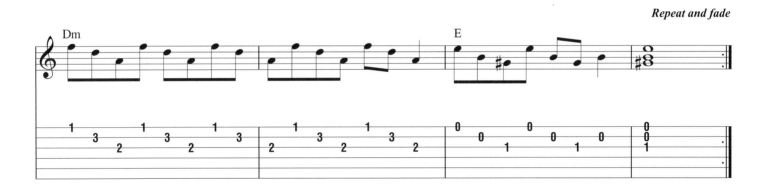

Additional Lyrics

2. Her mind is Tiffany twisted. She got the Mercedes bends.
   She got a lot of pretty, pretty boys that she calls friends.
   How they dance in the courtyard; sweet summer sweat.
   Some dance to remember; some dance to forget.
   So I called up the captain: "Please bring me my wine."
   He said, "We haven't had that spirit here since nineteen sixty-nine."
   And still those voices are calling from far away;
   Wake you up in the middle of the night just to hear them say:

3. Mirrors on the ceiling, the pink champagne on ice,
   And she said, "We are all just prisoners here of our own device."
   And in the master's chambers, they gathered for the feast.
   They stab it with their steely knives, but they just can't kill the beast.
   Last thing I remember, I was running for the door.
   I had to find the passage back to the place I was before.
   "Relax," said the night man. "We are programmed to receive.
   You can check out any time you like, but you can never leave."

Life in the Fast Lane

Words and Music by Don Henley, Glenn Frey and Joe Walsh

Strum Pattern: 1
Pick Pattern: 4

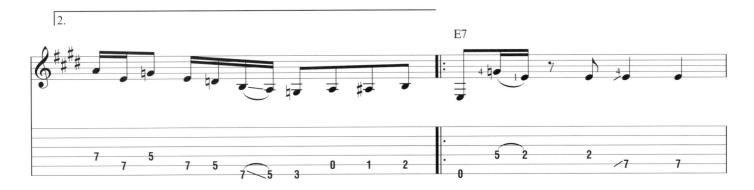

1. He was a

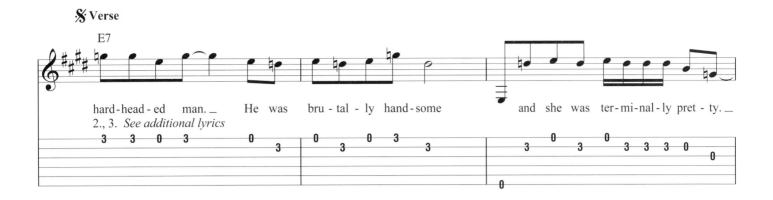

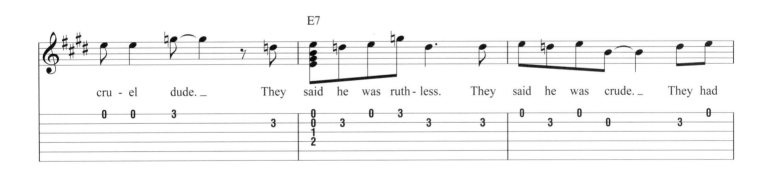

Chorus
w/ Intro riff

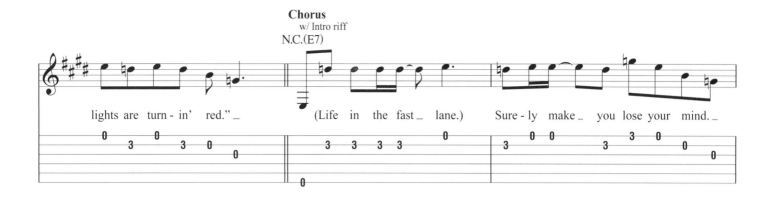

Guitar Solo

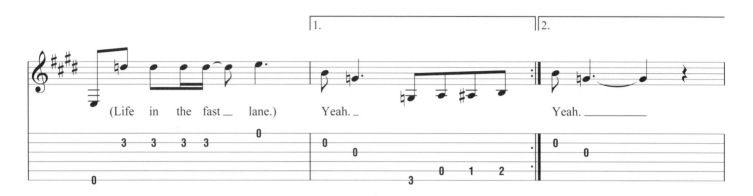

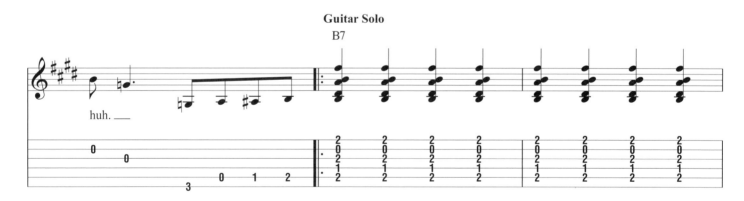

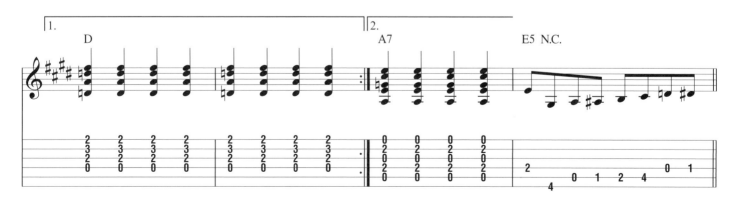

Additional Lyrics

2. Eager for action and hot for the game,
   The coming attraction, the drop of a name.
   They knew all the right people, they took all the right pills,
   They threw outrageous parties, they paid heavenly bills.
   There were lines on the mirror, lines on her face.
   She pretended not to notice, she was caught up in the race.
   Out ev'ry evening until it was light,
   He was too tired to make it, she was too tired to fight about it.

3. Blowin' and burnin', blinded by thirst,
   They didn't see the stop sign, took a turn for the worse.
   She said, "Listen, baby, you can hear the engine ring.
   We've been up and down this highway, haven't seen a goddamn thing."
   He said, "Call the doctor, I think I'm gonna crash."
   "The doctor say he's comin', but you gotta pay him cash."
   They went rushin' down that freeway, messed around and got lost.
   They didn't care, they were just dyin' to get off and it was...

The Long Run

Words and Music by Don Henley and Glenn Frey

Strum Pattern: 3, 1
Pick Pattern: 3

Intro
Moderately

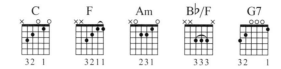

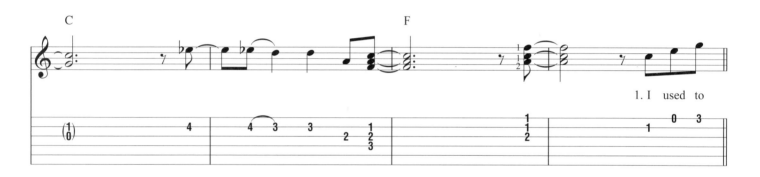

1. I used to

Verse

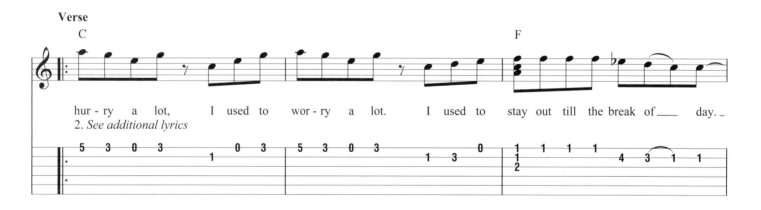

hur - ry a lot, I used to wor - ry a lot. I used to stay out till the break of ___ day. ___
2. *See additional lyrics*

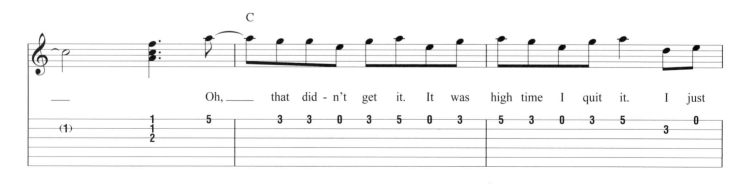

Oh, ___ that did - n't get it. It was high time I quit it. I just

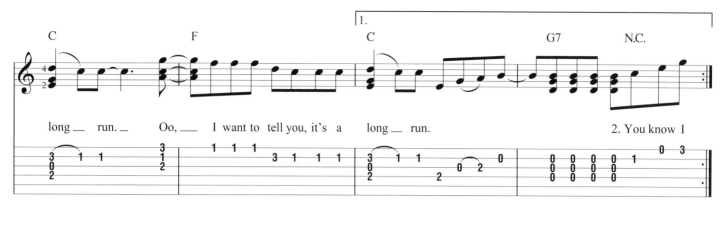

long __ run. __ Oo, __ I want to tell you, it's a long __ run. 2. You know I

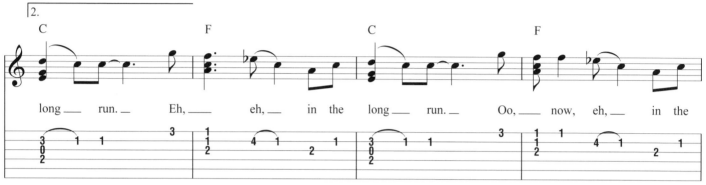

long __ run. __ Eh, __ eh, __ in the long __ run. Oo, __ now, eh, __ in the

Outro
w/ vocal ad lib.

long __ run. __

Repeat and fade

*Tie into beat 1.

Additional Lyrics

2. You know I don't understand why you don't treat yourself better, do the crazy things that you do.
   'Cause all the debutantes in Houston, baby, couldn't hold a candle to you.

Pre-Chorus Did you do it for love? Did you do it for money? Did you do it for spite? Did you think you had to, honey?

Chorus Who is gonna make it? We'll find out in the long run. (In the long run.)
I know we can take it if our love is a strong one. (Is a strong one.)
Well, we're scared, but we ain't shakin'. Kind of bent, but we ain't breakin' in the long run.
Oo, I want to tell you, it's a long run. Eh, eh, in the long run. Oo, now, eh, in the long run.

Lyin' Eyes

Words and Music by Don Henley and Glenn Frey

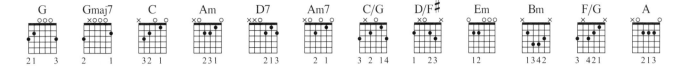

Strum Pattern: 2
Pick Pattern: 4

Intro
Moderately fast

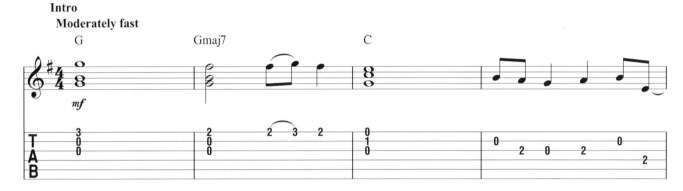

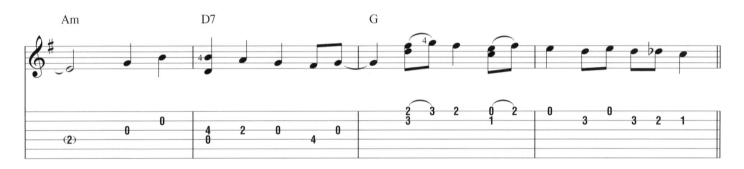

Verse

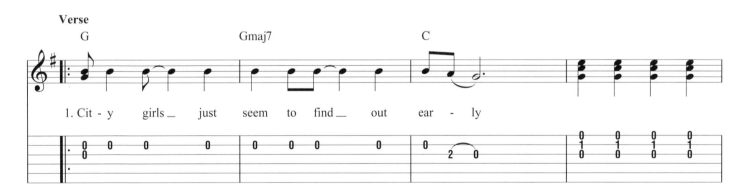

1. Cit - y girls _ just seem to find _ out ear - ly

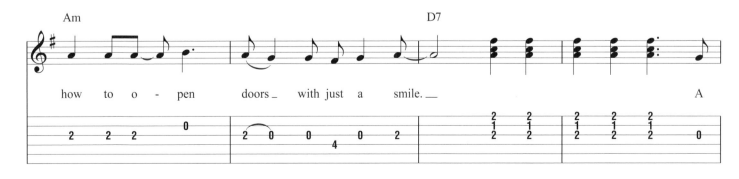

how to o - pen doors _ with just a smile. _

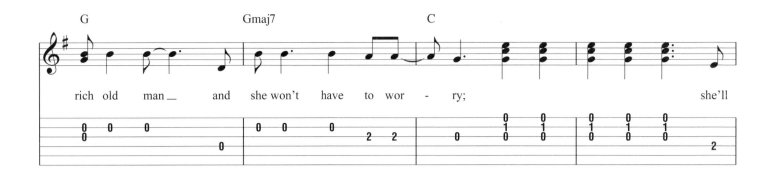

rich old man ___ and she won't have to wor - ry; she'll

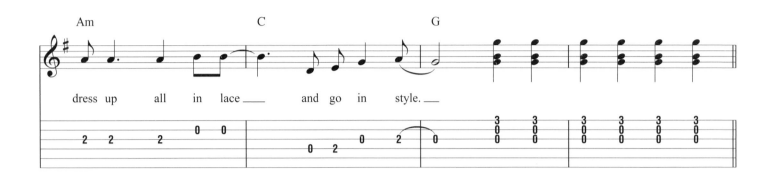

dress up all in lace ___ and go in style. ___

𝄋 Verse

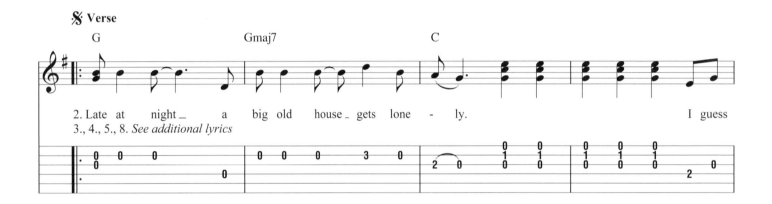

2. Late at night ___ a big old house ___ gets lone - ly. I guess
3., 4., 5., 8. *See additional lyrics*

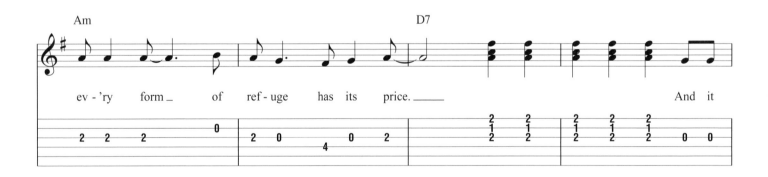

ev - 'ry form ___ of ref - uge has its price. ___ And it

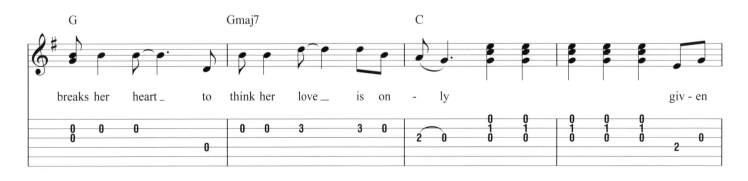

breaks her heart ___ to think her love ___ is on - ly giv - en

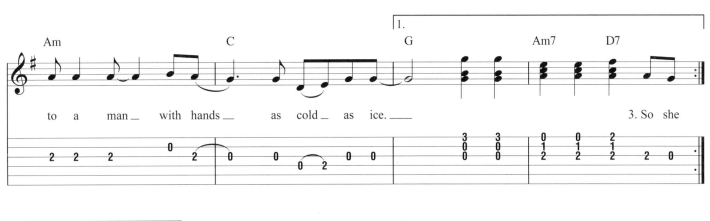

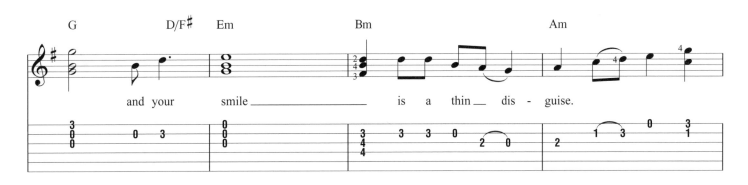

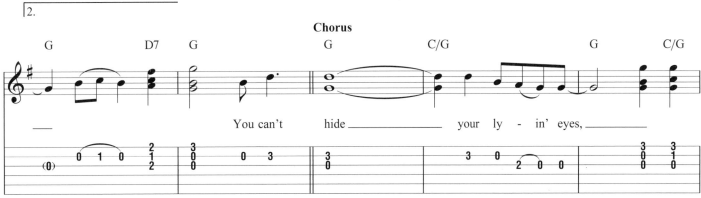

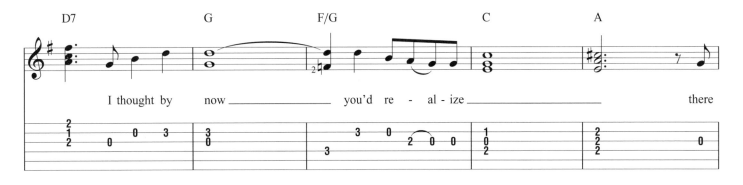

3rd time, to Coda 2

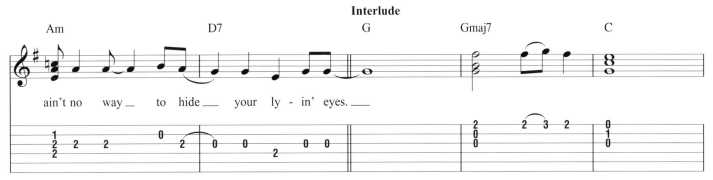

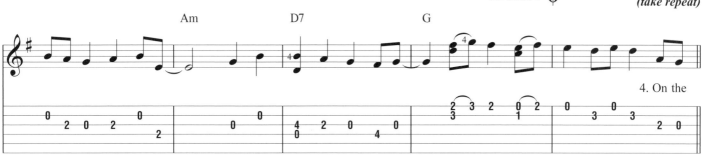

⊕ **Coda 1**

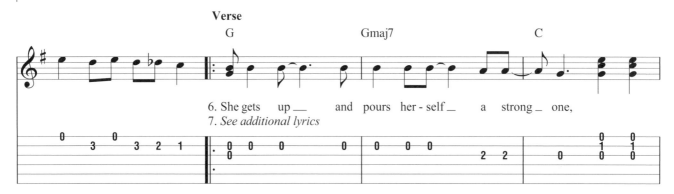

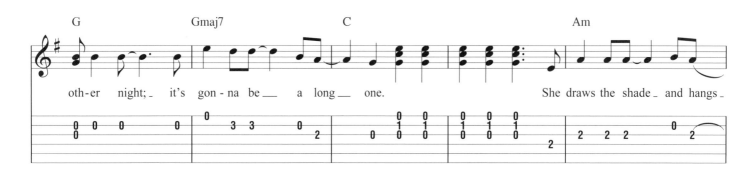

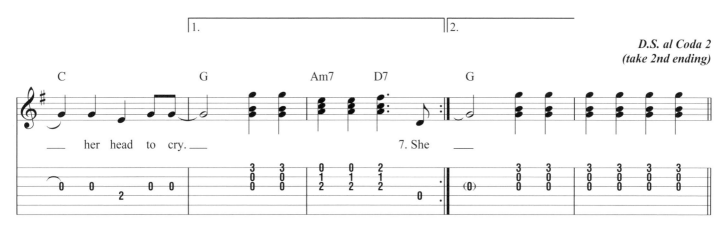

Coda 2

There ain't no way ___ to hide ___ your ly - in' eyes. ___

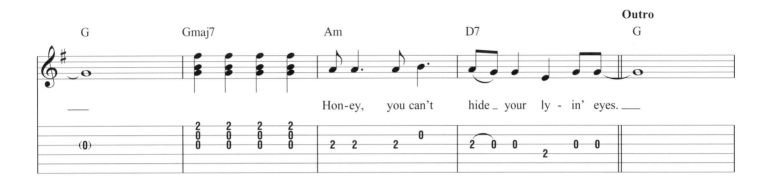

Outro

Hon-ey, you can't hide ___ your ly - in' eyes. ___

Freely

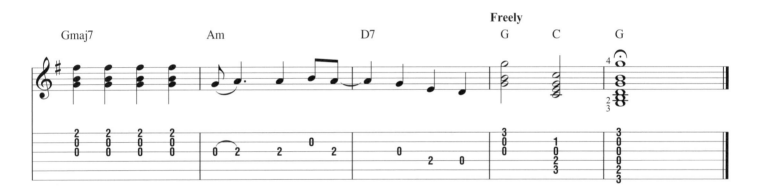

Additional Lyrics

3. So she tells him she must go out for the evening
   To comfort an old friend who's feelin' down.
   But he knows where she's goin' as she's leavin';
   She is headed for the cheatin' side of town.

4. On the other side of town a boy is waiting
   With fiery eyes and dreams no one could steal.
   She drives on through the night anticipating,
   'Cause he makes her feel the way she used to feel.

5. She rushes to his arms, they fall together.
   She whispers that it's only for a while.
   She swears that soon she'll be comin' back forever;
   She pulls away and leaves him with a smile.

7. She wonders how it ever got this crazy;
   She thinks about a boy she knew in school.
   Did she get tired or did she just get lazy?
   She's so far gone she feels just like a fool.

8. My, oh my, you sure know how to arrange things;
   You set it up so well, so carefully.
   Ain't it funny how your new life didn't change things;
   You're still the same old girl you used to be.

New Kid in Town

Words and Music by John David Souther, Don Henley and Glenn Frey

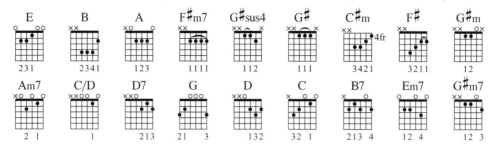

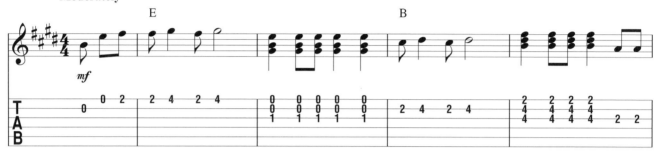

Strum Pattern: 1, 2
Pick Pattern: 2, 4

Intro
Moderately

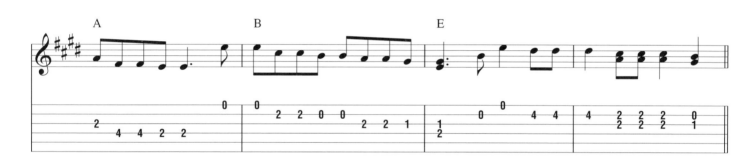

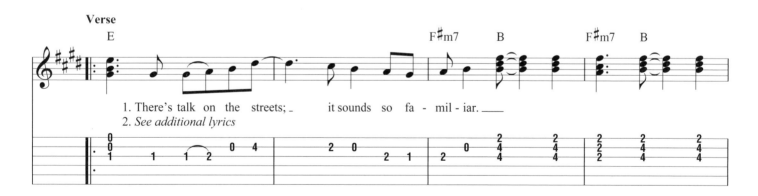

Verse

1. There's talk on the streets; _ it sounds so fa - mil - iar. ___
2. *See additional lyrics*

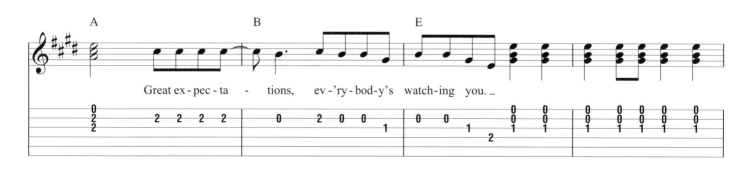

Great ex - pec - ta - tions, ev - 'ry - bod - y's watch - ing you. _

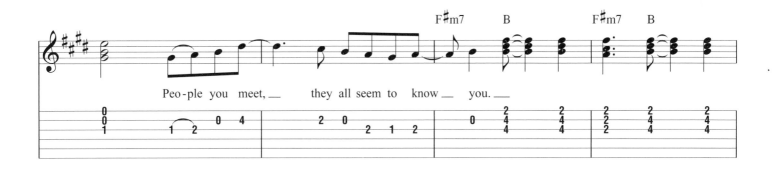

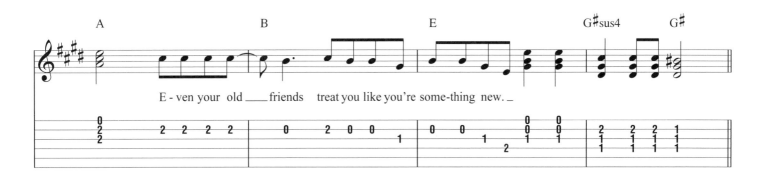

Chorus

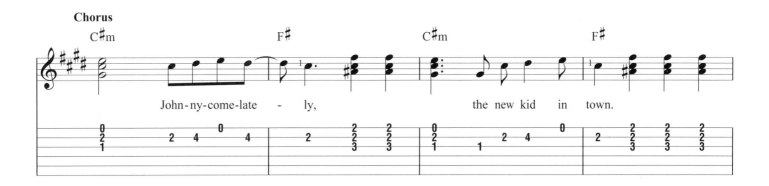

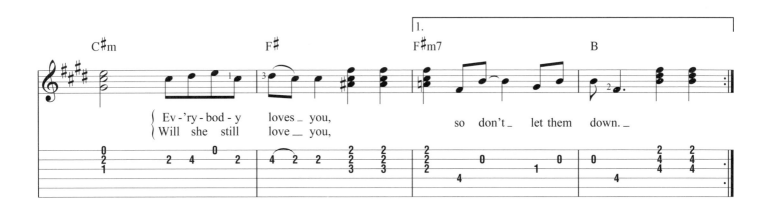

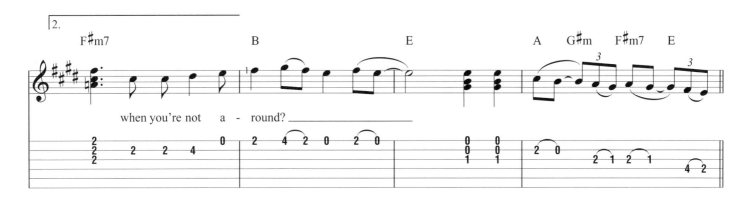

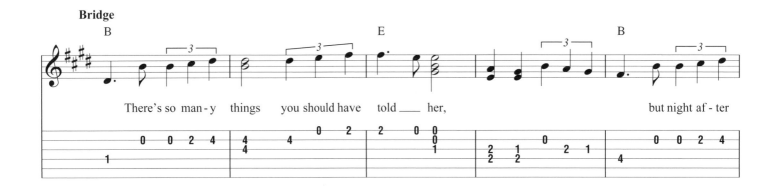

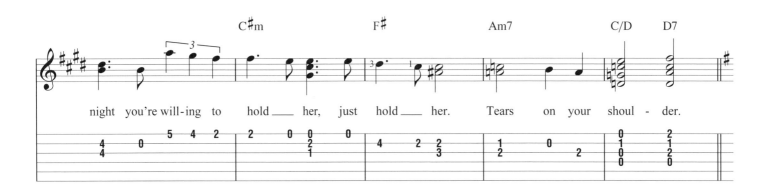

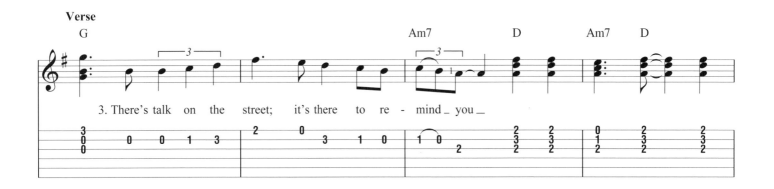

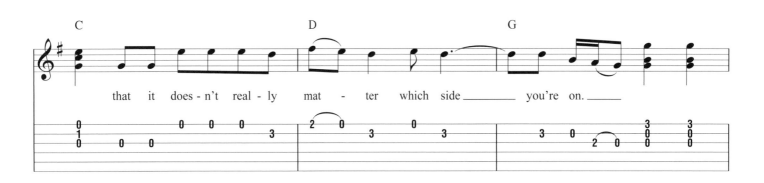

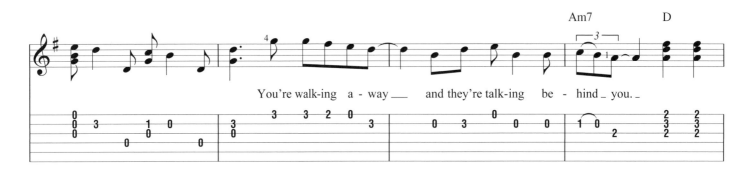

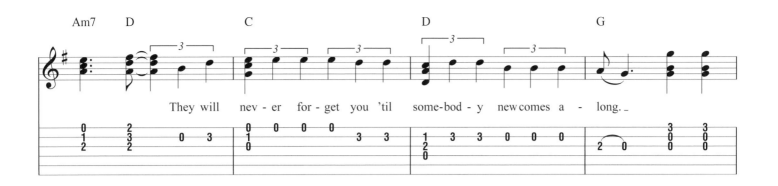

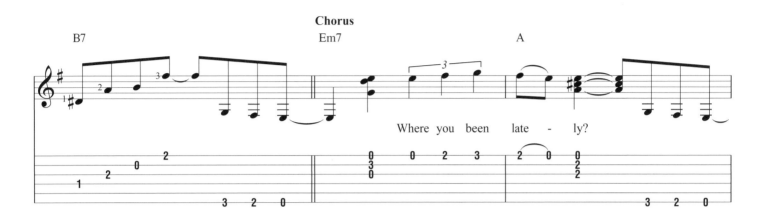

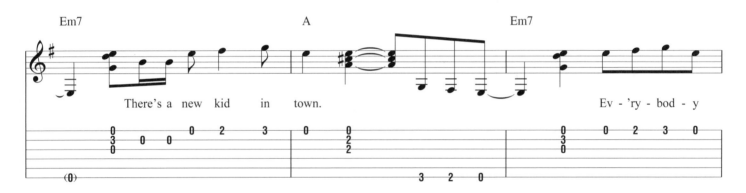

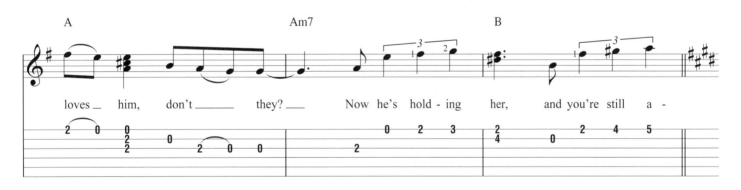

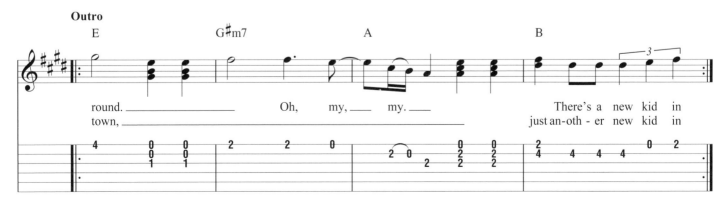

Additional Lyrics

2. You look in her eyes; the music begins to play.
Hopeless romantics, here we go again.
But after a while you're looking the other way.
It's those restless hearts that never mend.

One of These Nights

Words and Music by Don Henley and Glenn Frey

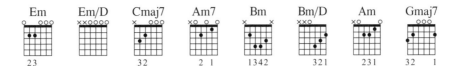

Strum Pattern: 5
Pick Pattern: 1

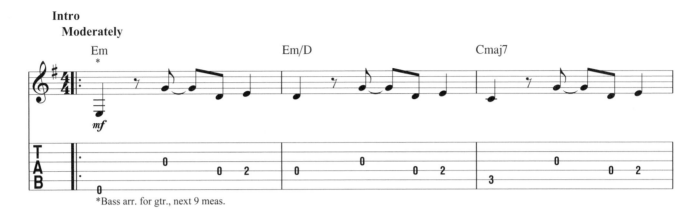

*Bass arr. for gtr., next 9 meas.

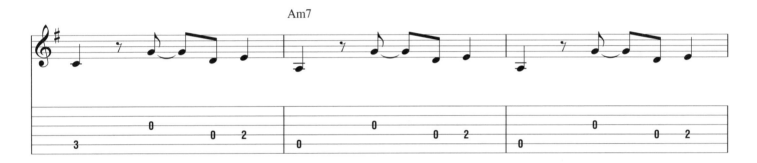

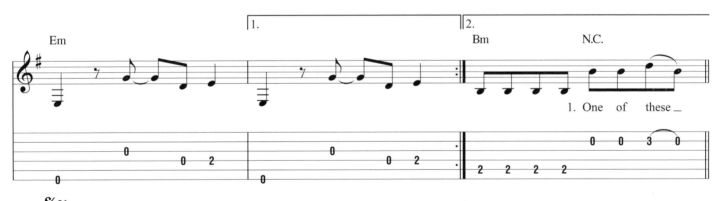

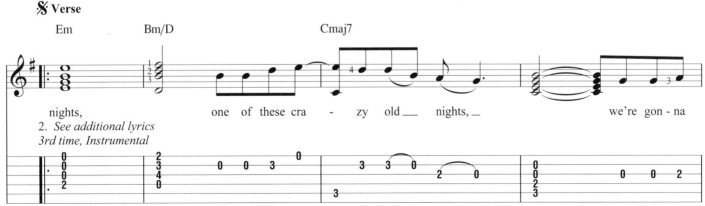

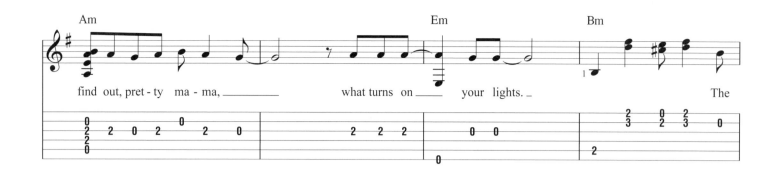

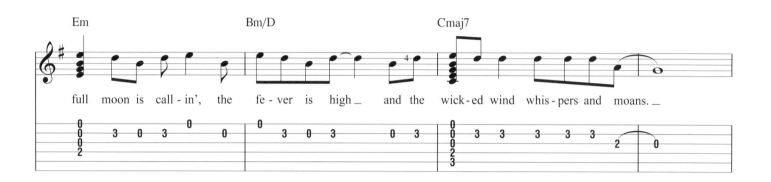

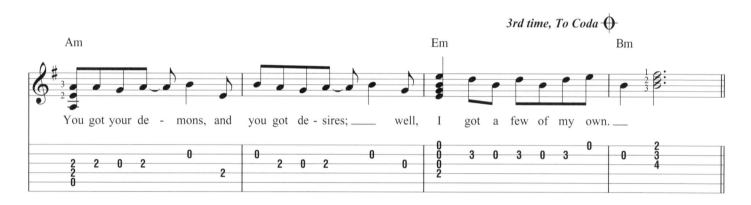

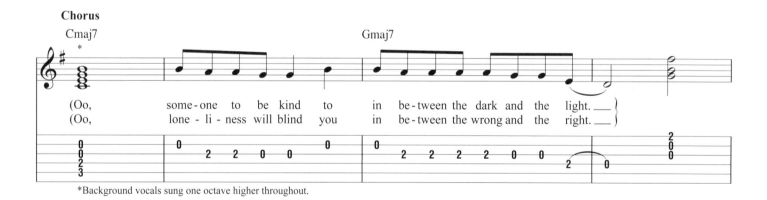

*Background vocals sung one octave higher throughout.

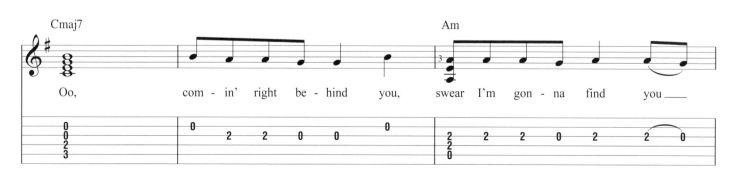

Additional Lyrics

Additional Lyrics

2. One of these dreams,
   One of these lost and lonely dreams, now,
   We're gonna find one, mm, one that really screams.
   I've been searchin' for the daughter of the devil himself,
   I've been searchin' for an angel in white.
   I've been waitin' for a woman who's a little of both,
   And I can feel her, but she's nowhere in sight.

Peaceful Easy Feeling

Words and Music by Jack Tempchin

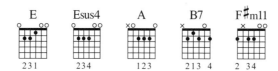

Strum Pattern: 2, 6
Pick Pattern: 6, 1

Intro
Moderately fast

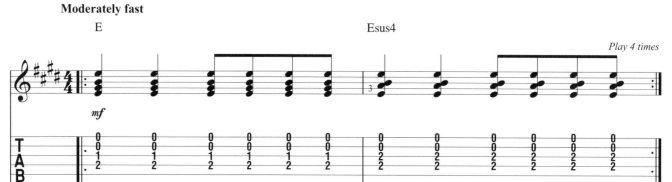

Play 4 times

Verse

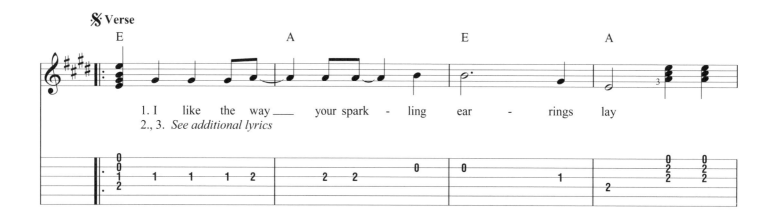

1. I like the way ___ your spark - ling ear - rings lay
2., 3. *See additional lyrics*

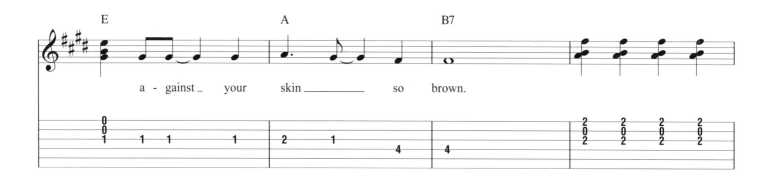

a - gainst ___ your skin _____ so brown.

And I wan - na sleep with you __ in the des - sert __ to - night, __

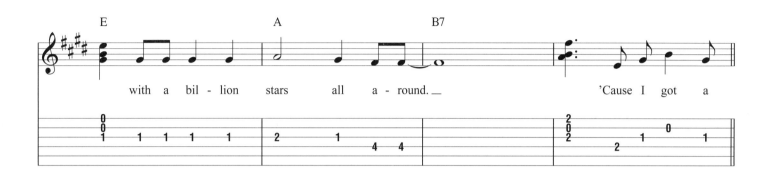

with a bil - lion stars all a - round. __ 'Cause I got a

Chorus

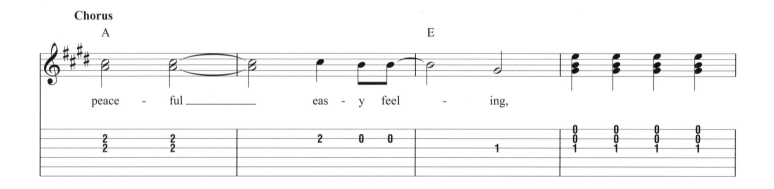

peace - ful _____ eas - y feel - ing,

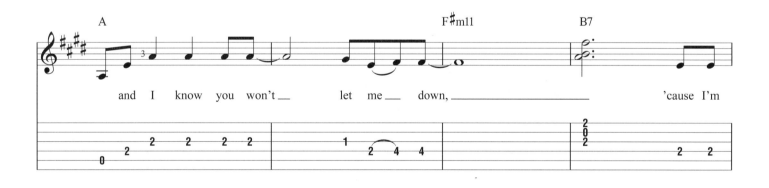

and I know you won't __ let me __ down, _____ 'cause I'm

To Coda ⊕

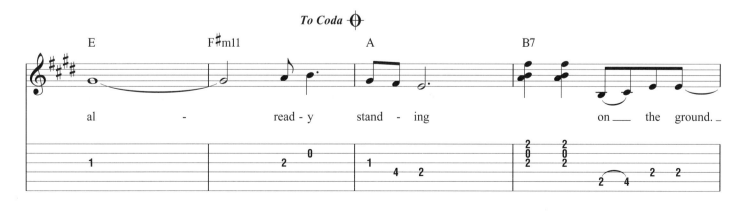

al - read - y stand - ing on __ the ground. __

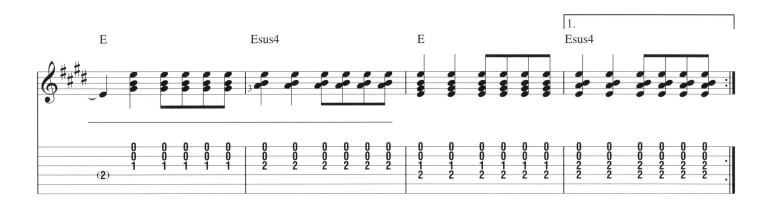

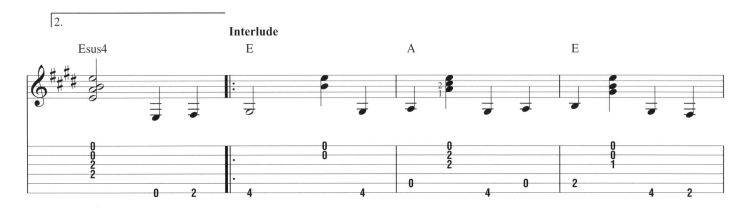

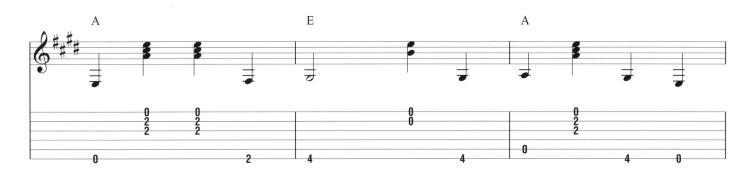

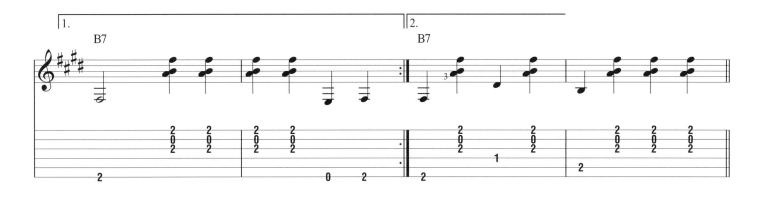

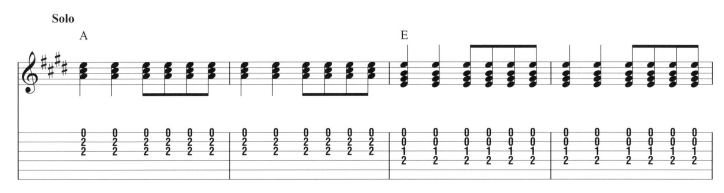

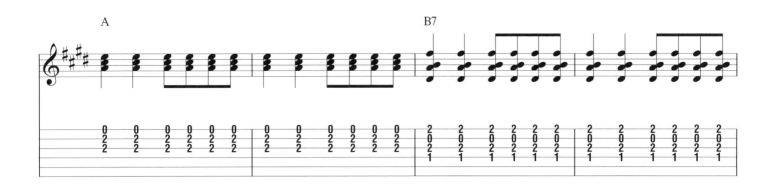

D.S. al Coda

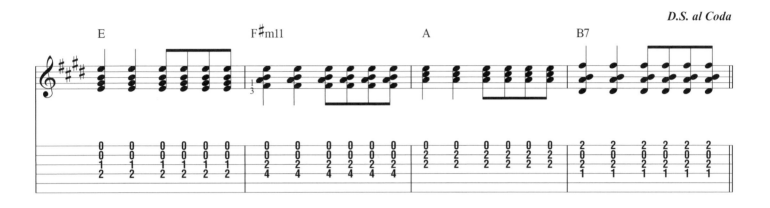

Coda

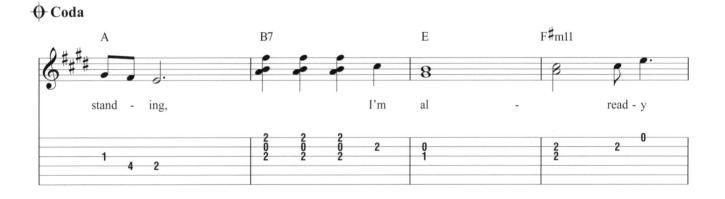

stand - ing,   I'm al - read - y

stand - ing, ___   yes, I'm al - read - y

Outro

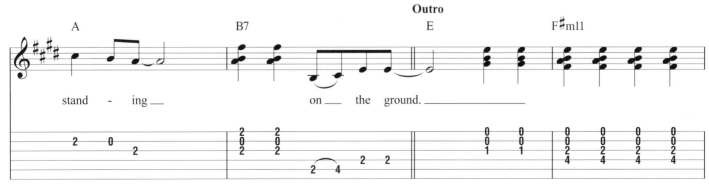

stand - ing ___   on ___ the ground. ___

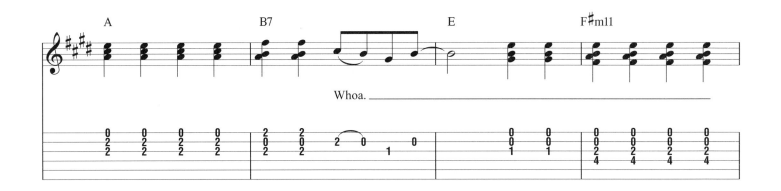

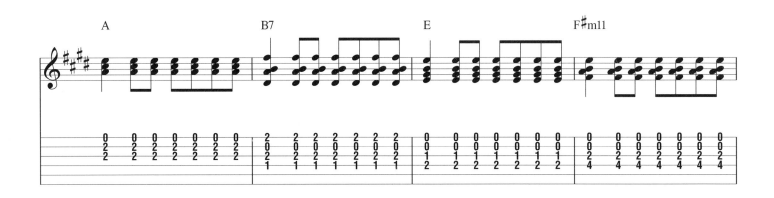

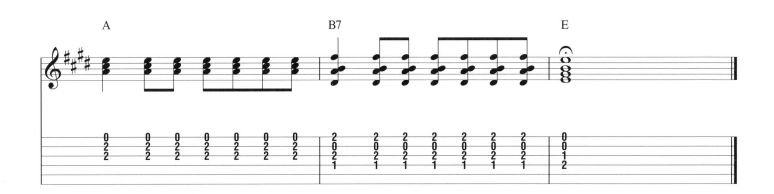

Additional Lyrics

2. And I found out a long time ago
   What a woman can do to your soul.
   Aw, but she can't take you anyway;
   You don't already know how to go.
   And I got a...

3. I get this feeling I may know you
   As a lover and a friend.
   But this voice keeps whispering in my other ear,
   Tells me I may never see you again.
   'Cause I get a...

Take It Easy

Words and Music by Jackson Browne and Glenn Frey

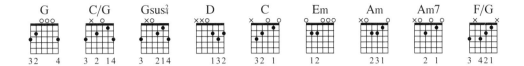

Strum Pattern: 2, 5
Pick Pattern: 1

Intro
Moderately fast

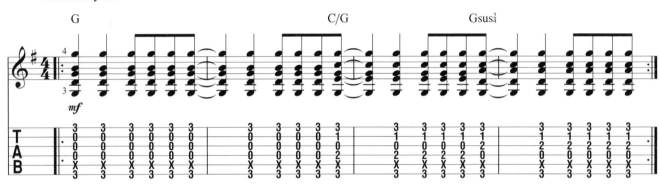

%. Verse

1. Well, I'm a run-nin' down the road try'n' to loos-en my load, _ I've got sev-
3. *See additional lyrics*

- en wom-en on my mind. Four that wan-na own me, two ___ that wan-na stone me,

*2nd time, substitute Am7

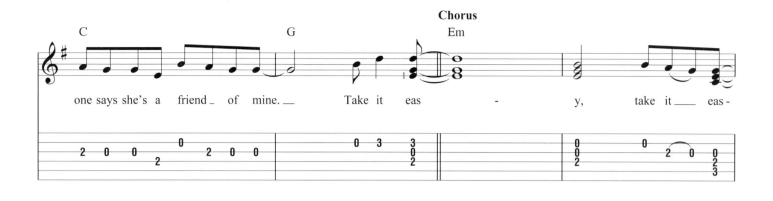

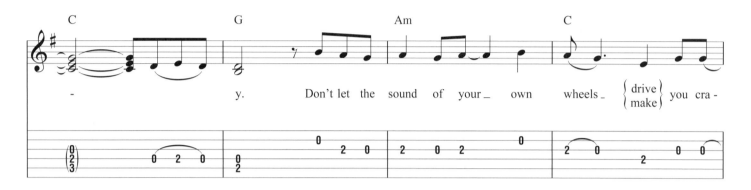

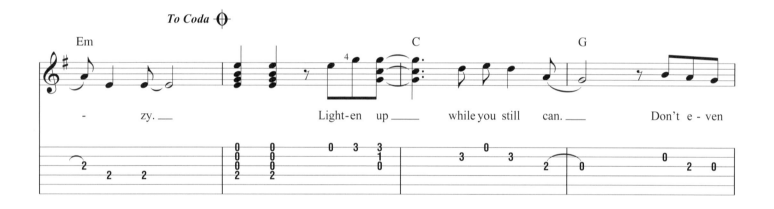

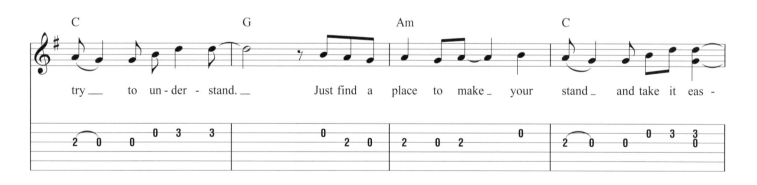

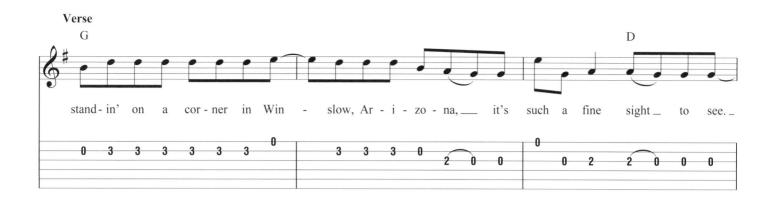

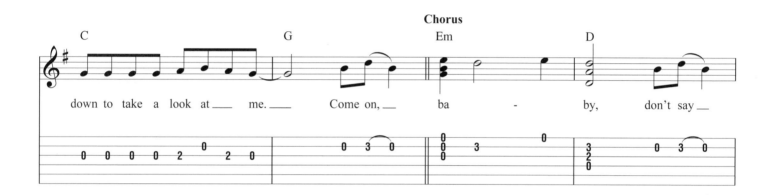

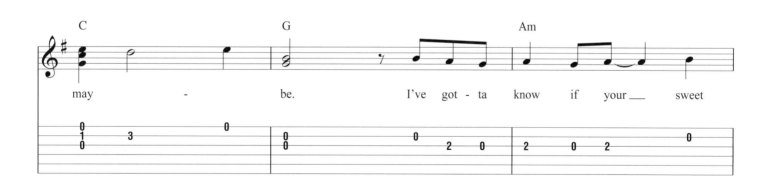

and we may win, though we will nev-er be here __ a-gain. __ So o-pen

D.S. al Coda

up, I'm climb-in' in, __ so take it eas - y. __ 3. Well, I'm a

Coda

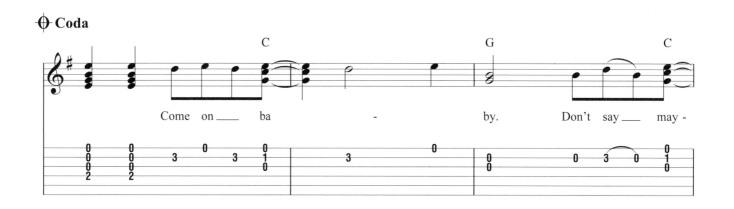

Come on __ ba - by. Don't say __ may-

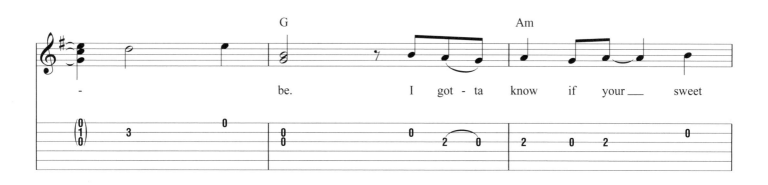

- be. I got-ta know if your __ sweet

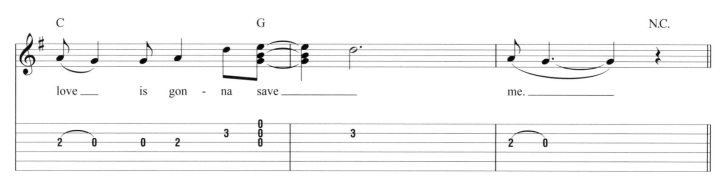

love __ is gon - na save __ me. __

Outro

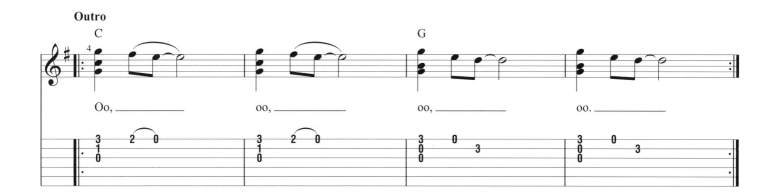

Oo, _____ oo, _____ oo, _____ oo. _____

Oo. _____ Oh, __ we got it eas -

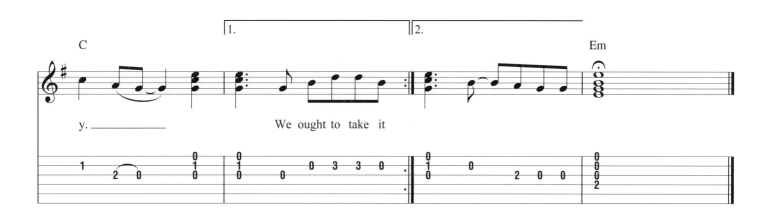

y. _____ We ought to take it

Additional Lyrics

3. Well, I'm a runnin' down the road try'n' to loosen my load,
   Got a world of trouble on my mind.
   Lookin' for a lover who won't blow my cover;
   She's so hard to find.

Tequila Sunrise

Words and Music by Don Henley and Glenn Frey

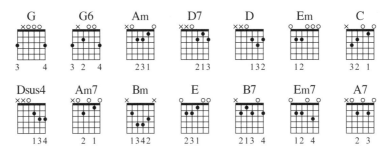

Strum Pattern: 2
Pick Pattern: 4

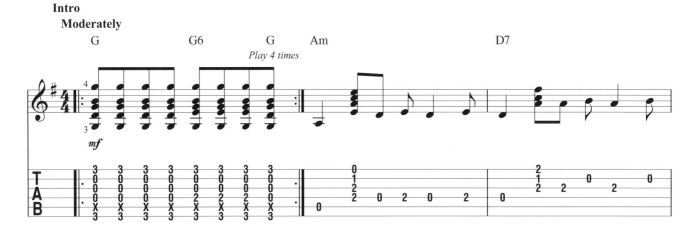

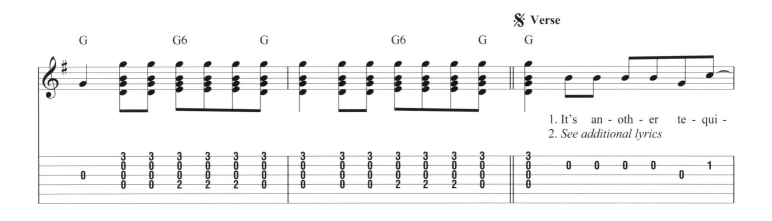

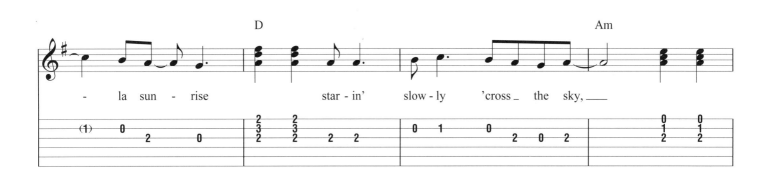

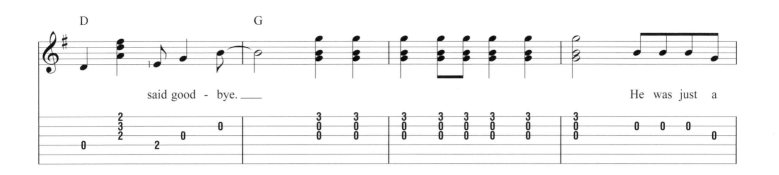

said good - bye. ____   He was just a

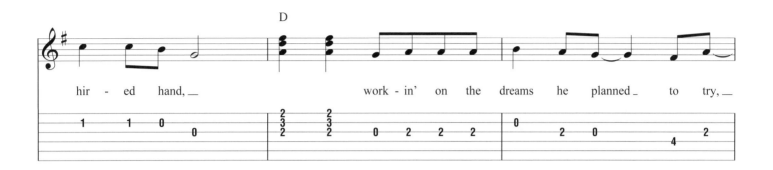

hir - ed hand, ____   work - in' on the dreams he planned __ to try, __

To Coda

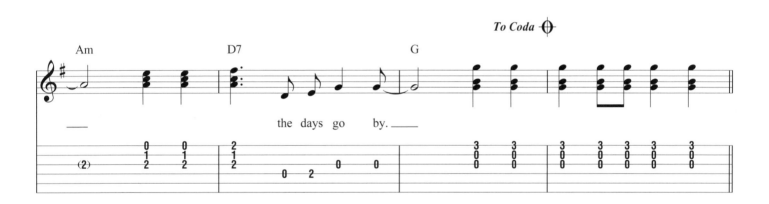

____   the days go   by. ____

Chorus

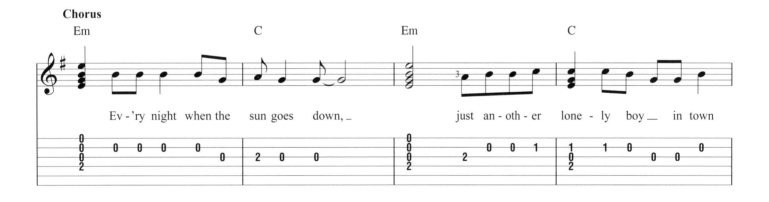

Ev - 'ry night when the   sun goes   down, _   just an - oth - er   lone - ly boy __ in town

D.S. al Coda

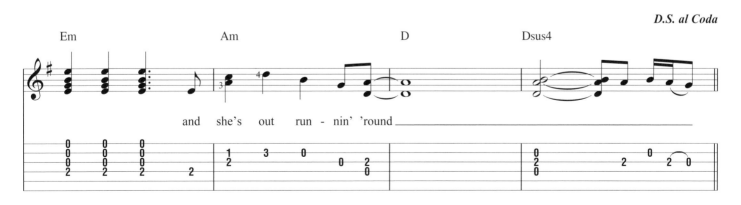

and she's out run - nin' 'round _____

Interlude

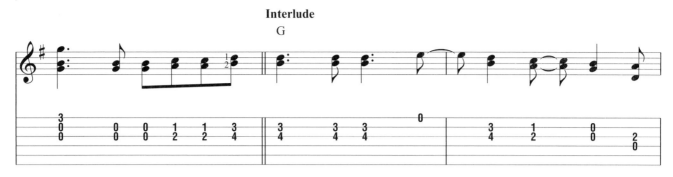

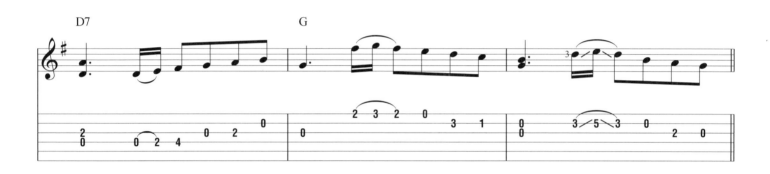

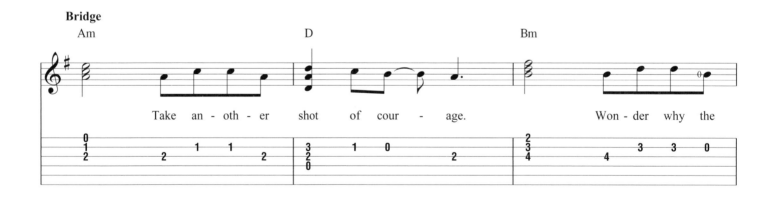

Bridge

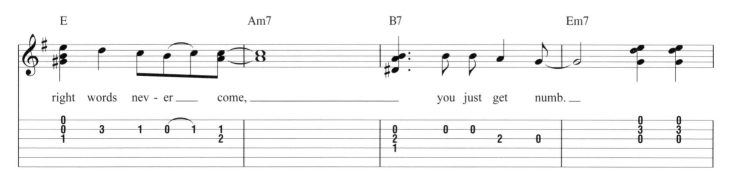

Take an-oth-er shot of cour - age. Won-der why the

right words nev-er ___ come, _____ you just get numb. ___

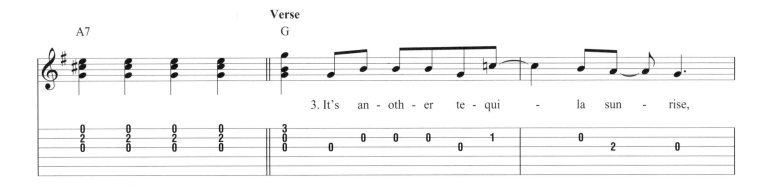

3. It's an - oth - er te - qui - la sun - rise,

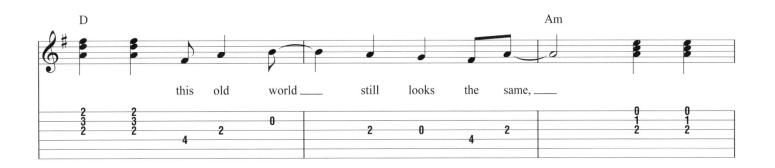

this old world ___ still looks the same, ___

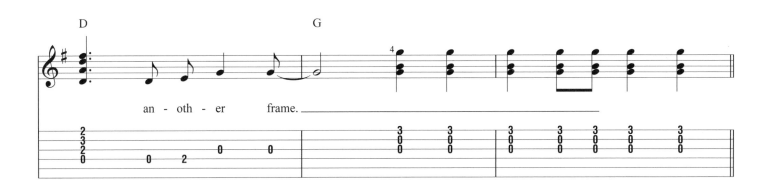

an - oth - er frame. _____

Outro

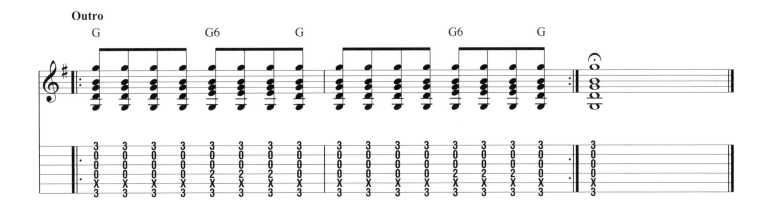

Additional Lyrics

2. She wasn't just another woman and I couldn't keep from coming on,
   Been so long.
   Whoa, and it's a hollow feeling when it comes down to dealin' friends,
   It never ends.

Witchy Woman

Words and Music by Don Henley and Bernie Leadon

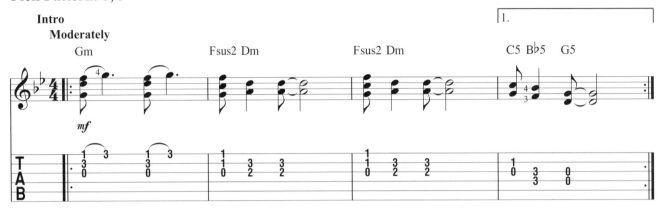

Strum Pattern: 1, 3
Pick Pattern: 5, 3

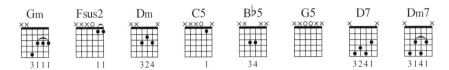

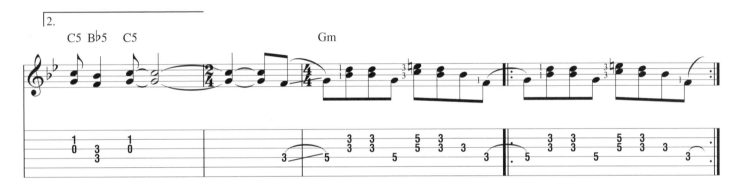

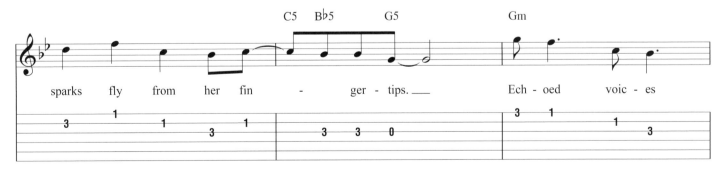

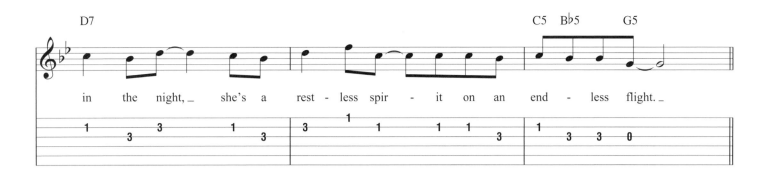

in the night, _ she's a rest - less spir - it on an end - less flight. _

Chorus

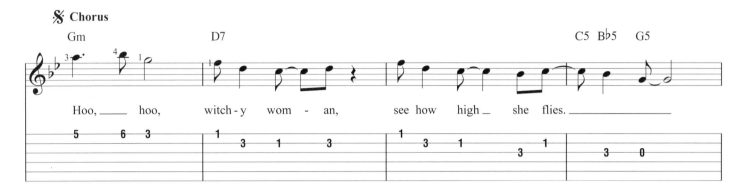

Hoo, _ hoo, witch-y wom - an, see how high _ she flies. _____

To Coda ⊕

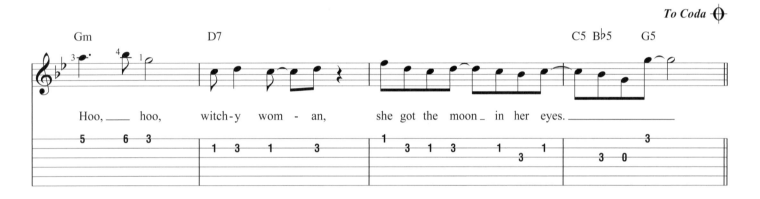

Hoo, _ hoo, witch-y wom - an, she got the moon _ in her eyes. _____

1.

Interlude

2. She

2.

Interlude

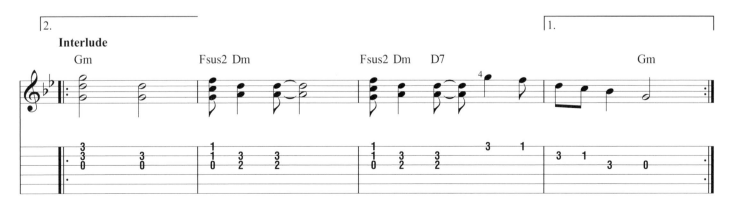

let me tell you, broth - er, she's been sleep - ing in the dev - il's bed. ____ And there's some

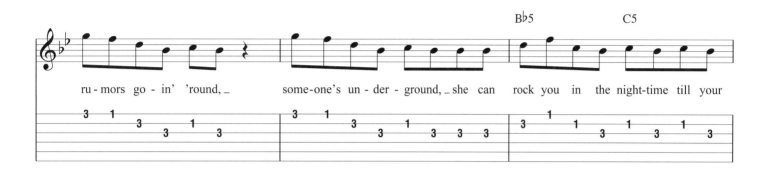

ru - mors go - in' 'round, _ some-one's un - der - ground, _ she can rock you in the night-time till your

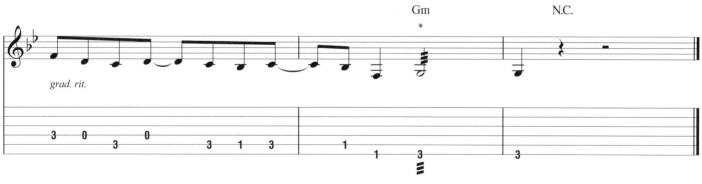

D.S. al Coda

Coda

Outro

skin turns red. ____

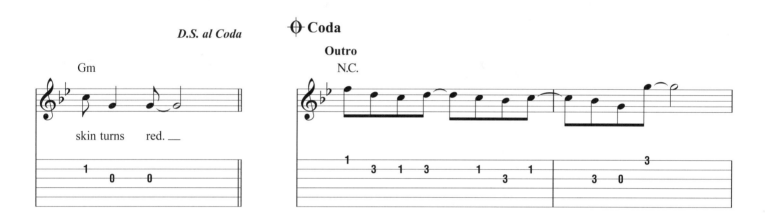

grad. rit.

*Tremolo picking: Pick the note as
rapidly and continously as possible.

Additional Lyrics

2. She held me spellbound in the night,
   Dancing shadows an' firelight.
   Crazy laughter in another room,
   An' she drove herself to madness with a silver spoon.

You Never Cry Like a Lover

Words and Music by John David Souther and Don Henley

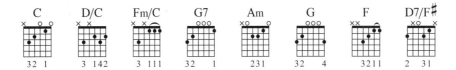

Strum Pattern: 2
Pick Pattern: 4

Intro
Moderately slow

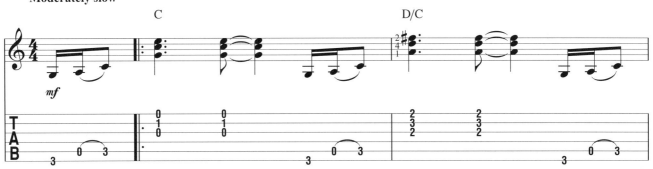

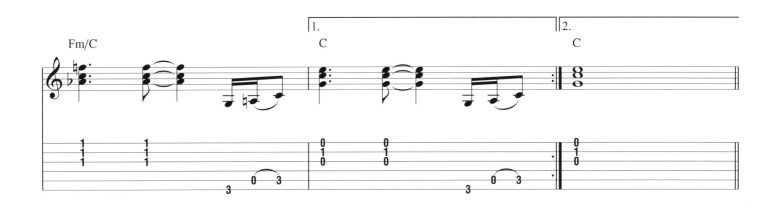

% Chorus

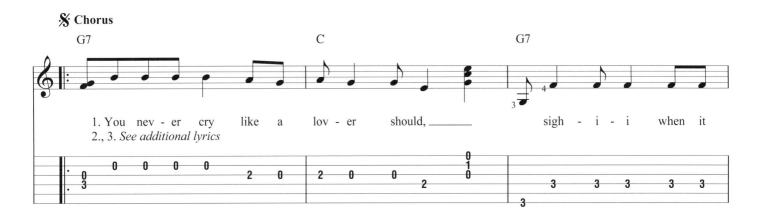

1. You nev-er cry like a lov-er should, _____ sigh - i - i when it
2., 3. *See additional lyrics*

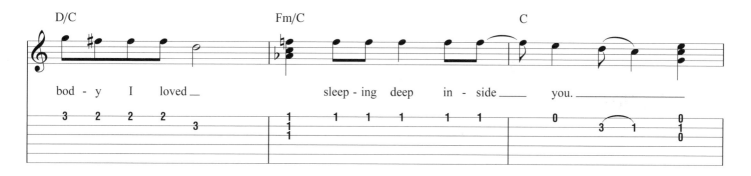

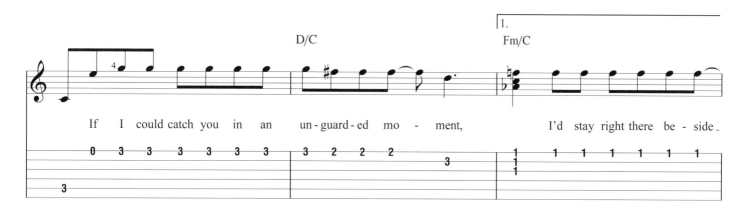

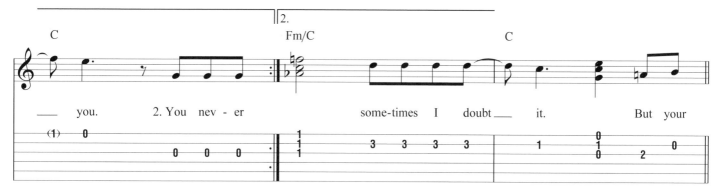

Bridge

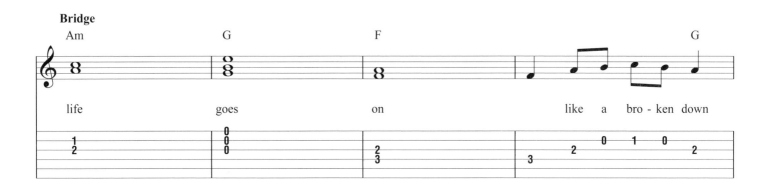

life   goes   on   like a bro - ken down

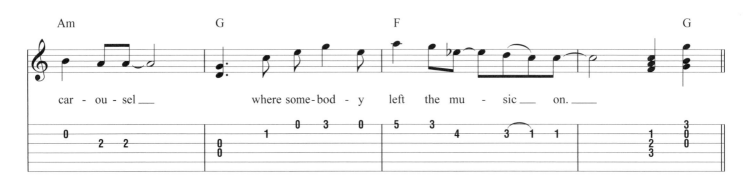

car - ou - sel ___   where some-bod - y   left   the mu - sic ___   on. ___

Interlude

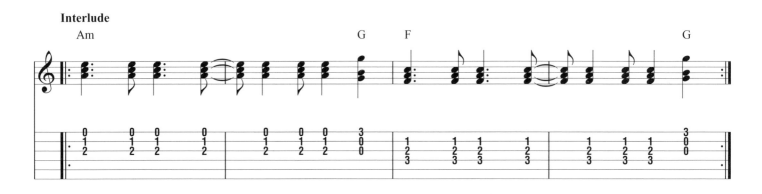

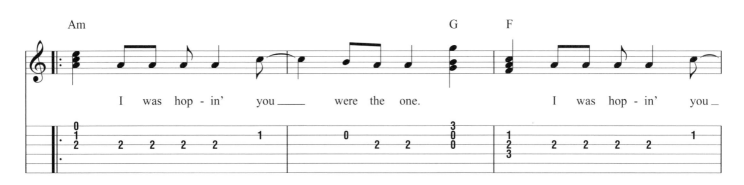

I was hop - in' you ___   were the one.   I was hop - in' you ___

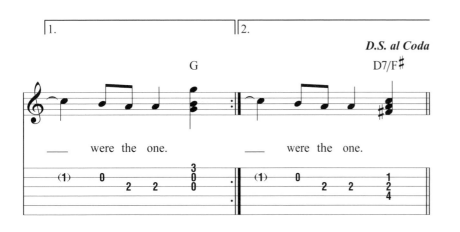

1.   2.   *D.S. al Coda*   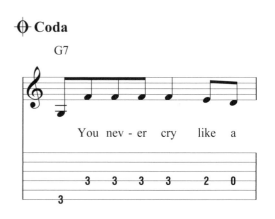 **Coda**

___ were the one.   ___ were the one.   You nev - er cry like a

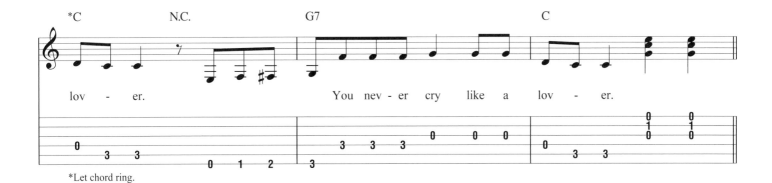

*C   N.C.   G7   C

lov - er.   You nev - er cry like a lov - er.

*Let chord ring.

Outro

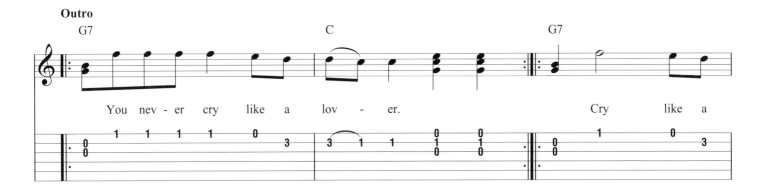

G7   C   G7

You nev - er cry like a lov - er.   Cry like a

Repeat and fade

C   G7   C

lov - er.   You nev - er cry like a lov - er.

Additional Lyrics

Chorus 2. You never smile at me late at night,
Laugh out loud when we get it right.
You can't get loose if there's too much light.
You never smile like a lover.

     2. I can't live with you, baby,
Can't live without it.
And sometimes I believe in love,
Sometimes I doubt it.

Chorus 3. You never move like you used to,
Pour it out when you're feelin' blue.
Somebody must have put some pain on you.
You never cry like a lover.
You never cry like a lover.

Take It to the Limit

Words and Music by Don Henley, Glenn Frey and Randy Meisner

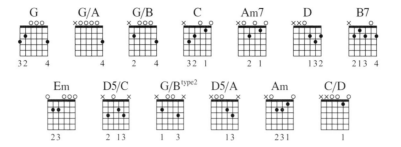

*Capo IV

Strum Pattern: 8, 9
Pick Pattern: 8

Intro
Moderately slow

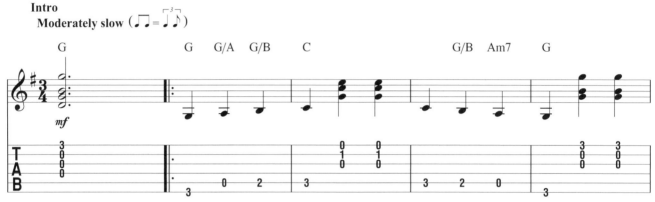

*Optional: To match recording, place capo at 4th fret.

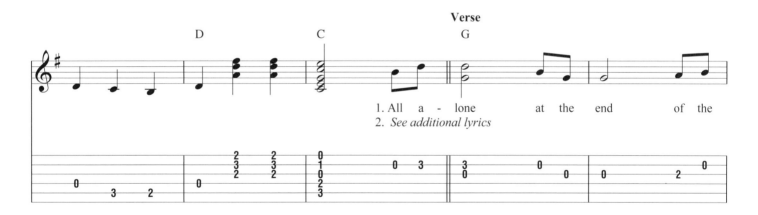

1. All a - lone   at the end   of the
2. *See additional lyrics*

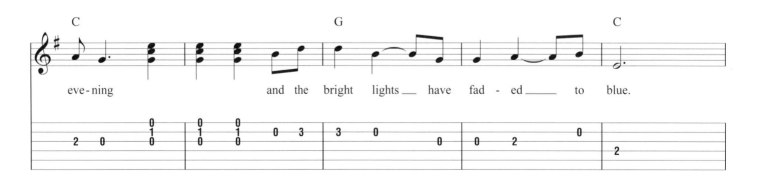

eve - ning   and the bright lights ___ have fad - ed ___ to blue.

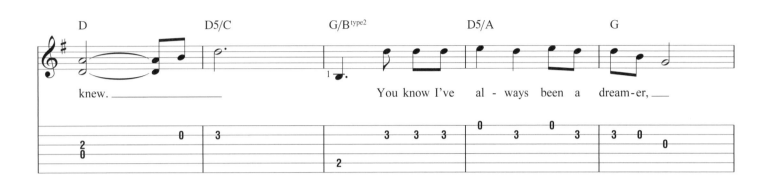

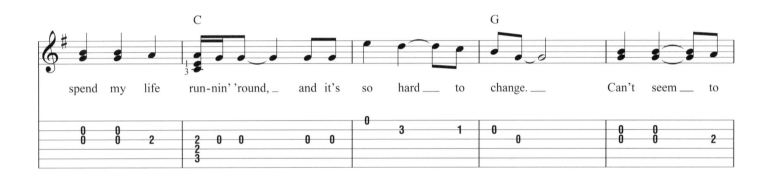

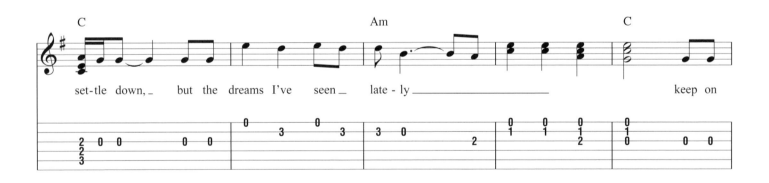

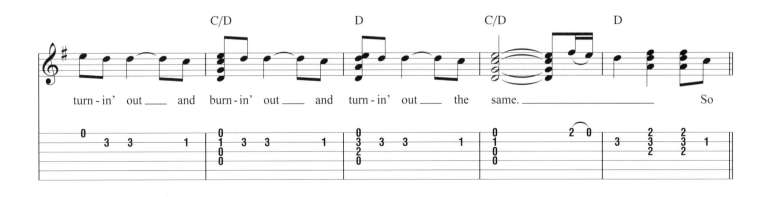

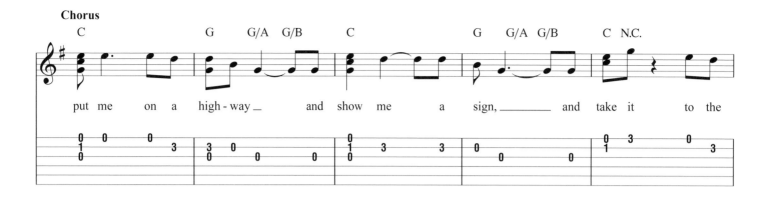

put me on a high-way __ and show me a sign, _____ and take it to the

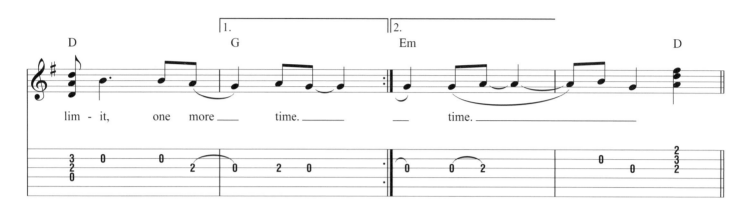

lim - it, one more ____ time. _____ ___ time. _____

Outro-Chorus

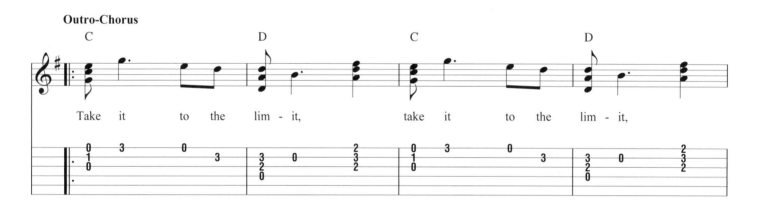

Take it to the lim - it, take it to the lim - it,

Repeat and fade

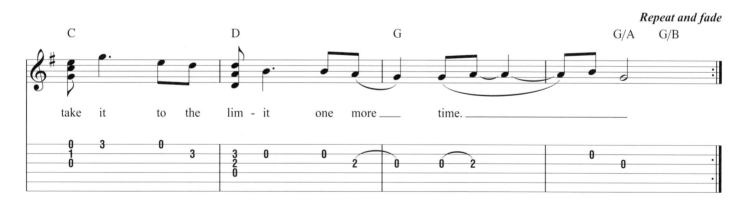

take it to the lim - it one more ____ time. _____

Additional Lyrics

2. You can spend all your time making money.
   You can spend all your love making time.
   If it all fell to pieces tomorrow
   Would you still be mine?
   And when you're lookin' for your freedom,
   Nobody seems to care.
   And you can't find the door,
   Can't find it anywhere.
   When there's nothing to believe in,
   Still you're comin' back, you're runnin' back for more.

This series features simplified arrangements with notes, tab, chord charts, and strum and pick patterns.

MIXED FOLIOS

00702287	Acoustic	$19.99
00702002	Acoustic Rock Hits for Easy Guitar	$17.99
00702166	All-Time Best Guitar Collection	$29.99
00702232	Best Acoustic Songs for Easy Guitar	$16.99
00119835	Best Children's Songs	$16.99
00703055	The Big Book of Nursery Rhymes & Children's Songs	$16.99
00698978	Big Christmas Collection	$19.99
00702394	Bluegrass Songs for Easy Guitar	$15.99
00289632	Bohemian Rhapsody	$19.99
00703387	Celtic Classics	$16.99
00224808	Chart Hits of 2016-2017	$14.99
00267383	Chart Hits of 2017-2018	$14.99
00334293	Chart Hits of 2019-2020	$16.99
00403479	Chart Hits of 2021-2022	$16.99
00702149	Children's Christian Songbook	$9.99
00702028	Christmas Classics	$9.99
00101779	Christmas Guitar	$16.99
00702141	Classic Rock	$8.95
00159642	Classical Melodies	$12.99
00253933	Disney/Pixar's Coco	$19.99
00702203	CMT's 100 Greatest Country Songs	$34.99
00702283	The Contemporary Christian Collection	$16.99

00196954	Contemporary Disney	$19.99
00702239	Country Classics for Easy Guitar	$24.99
00702257	Easy Acoustic Guitar Songs	$17.99
00702041	Favorite Hymns for Easy Guitar	$12.99
00222701	Folk Pop Songs	$19.99
00126894	Frozen	$14.99
00333922	Frozen 2	$14.99
00702286	Glee	$16.99
00702160	The Great American Country Songbook	$19.99
00702148	Great American Gospel for Guitar	$14.99
00702050	Great Classical Themes for Easy Guitar	$9.99
00148030	Halloween Guitar Songs	$17.99
00702273	Irish Songs	$14.99
00192503	Jazz Classics for Easy Guitar	$16.99
00702275	Jazz Favorites for Easy Guitar	$17.99
00702274	Jazz Standards for Easy Guitar	$19.99
00702162	Jumbo Easy Guitar Songbook	$24.99
00232285	La La Land	$16.99
00702258	Legends of Rock	$14.99
00702189	MTV's 100 Greatest Pop Songs	$34.99
00702272	1950s Rock	$16.99
00702271	1960s Rock	$16.99
00702270	1970s Rock	$24.99
00702269	1980s Rock	$16.99

00702268	1990s Rock	$24.99
00369043	Rock Songs for Kids	$14.99
00109725	Once	$14.99
00702187	Selections from O Brother Where Art Thou?	$19.99
00702178	100 Songs for Kids	$16.99
00702515	Pirates of the Caribbean	$17.99
00702125	Praise and Worship for Guitar	$14.99
00287930	Songs from *A Star Is Born, The Greatest Showman, La La Land*, and More Movie Musicals	$16.99
00702285	Southern Rock Hits	$12.99
00156420	Star Wars Music	$16.99
00121535	30 Easy Celtic Guitar Solos	$16.99
00244654	Top Hits of 2017	$14.99
00283786	Top Hits of 2018	$14.99
00302269	Top Hits of 2019	$14.99
00355779	Top Hits of 2020	$14.99
00374083	Top Hits of 2021	$16.99
00702294	Top Worship Hits	$17.99
00702255	VH1's 100 Greatest Hard Rock Songs	$39.99
00702175	VH1's 100 Greatest Songs of Rock and Roll	$34.99
00702253	Wicked	$12.99

ARTIST COLLECTIONS

00702267	AC/DC for Easy Guitar	$17.99
00156221	Adele – 25	$16.99
00396889	Adele – 30	$19.99
00702040	Best of the Allman Brothers	$16.99
00702865	J.S. Bach for Easy Guitar	$15.99
00702169	Best of The Beach Boys	$16.99
00702292	The Beatles — 1	$22.99
00125796	Best of Chuck Berry	$16.99
00702201	The Essential Black Sabbath	$15.99
00702250	blink-182 — Greatest Hits	$19.99
02501615	Zac Brown Band — The Foundation	$19.99
02501621	Zac Brown Band — You Get What You Give	$16.99
00702043	Best of Johnny Cash	$19.99
00702090	Eric Clapton's Best	$16.99
00702086	Eric Clapton — from the Album Unplugged	$17.99
00702202	The Essential Eric Clapton	$19.99
00702053	Best of Patsy Cline	$17.99
00222697	Very Best of Coldplay – 2nd Edition	$17.99
00702229	The Very Best of Creedence Clearwater Revival	$16.99
00702145	Best of Jim Croce	$16.99
00702278	Crosby, Stills & Nash	$12.99
14042809	Bob Dylan	$15.99
00702276	Fleetwood Mac — Easy Guitar Collection	$17.99
00139462	The Very Best of Grateful Dead	$17.99
00702136	Best of Merle Haggard	$19.99
00702227	Jimi Hendrix — Smash Hits	$19.99
00702288	Best of Hillsong United	$12.99
00702236	Best of Antonio Carlos Jobim	$15.99

00702245	Elton John — Greatest Hits 1970–2002	$19.99
00129855	Jack Johnson	$17.99
00702204	Robert Johnson	$16.99
00702234	Selections from Toby Keith — 35 Biggest Hits	$12.95
00702003	Kiss	$16.99
00702216	Lynyrd Skynyrd	$17.99
00702182	The Essential Bob Marley	$17.99
00146081	Maroon 5	$14.99
00121925	Bruno Mars – Unorthodox Jukebox	$12.99
00702248	Paul McCartney — All the Best	$14.99
00125484	The Best of MercyMe	$12.99
00702209	Steve Miller Band — Young Hearts (Greatest Hits)	$12.95
00124167	Jason Mraz	$15.99
00702096	Best of Nirvana	$17.99
00702211	The Offspring — Greatest Hits	$17.99
00138026	One Direction	$17.99
00702030	Best of Roy Orbison	$17.99
00702144	Best of Ozzy Osbourne	$14.99
00702279	Tom Petty	$17.99
00102911	Pink Floyd	$17.99
00702139	Elvis Country Favorites	$19.99
00702293	The Very Best of Prince	$22.99
00699415	Best of Queen for Guitar	$16.99
00109279	Best of R.E.M.	$14.99
00702208	Red Hot Chili Peppers — Greatest Hits	$19.99
00198960	The Rolling Stones	$17.99
00174793	The Very Best of Santana	$16.99
00702196	Best of Bob Seger	$16.99
00146046	Ed Sheeran	$19.99

00702252	Frank Sinatra — Nothing But the Best	$12.99
00702010	Best of Rod Stewart	$17.99
00702049	Best of George Strait	$17.99
00702259	Taylor Swift for Easy Guitar	$15.99
00359800	Taylor Swift – Easy Guitar Anthology	$24.99
00702260	Taylor Swift — Fearless	$14.99
00139727	Taylor Swift — 1989	$19.99
00115960	Taylor Swift — Red	$16.99
00253667	Taylor Swift — Reputation	$17.99
00702290	Taylor Swift — Speak Now	$16.99
00232849	Chris Tomlin Collection – 2nd Edition	$14.99
00702226	Chris Tomlin — See the Morning	$12.95
00148643	Train	$14.99
00702427	U2 — 18 Singles	$19.99
00702108	Best of Stevie Ray Vaughan	$17.99
00279005	The Who	$14.99
00702123	Best of Hank Williams	$15.99
00194548	Best of John Williams	$14.99
00702228	Neil Young — Greatest Hits	$17.99
00119133	Neil Young — Harvest	$16.99

Prices, contents and availability subject to change without notice.

Visit Hal Leonard online at halleonard.com

HAL·LEONARD GUITAR PLAY-ALONG

Complete song lists available online.

This series will help you play your favorite songs quickly and easily. Just follow the tab and listen to the audio to the hear how the guitar should sound, and then play along using the separate backing tracks. Audio files also include software to slow down the tempo without changing pitch. The melody and lyrics are included in the book so that you can sing or simply follow along.

INCLUDES TAB

Prices, contents, and availability subject to change without notice.

www.halleonard.com